Final Fantasy VI

Sebastian Deken

Boss Fight Books
Los Angeles, CA
bossfightbooks.com

ISBN 13: 978-1-940535-28-9
First Printing: 2021

Series Editor: Gabe Durham
Associate Editor: Michael P. Williams
Book Design by Cory Schmitz
Page Design by Christopher Moyer

Final Fantasy VI

oh
my
god

Paula

where
did you get
that book

CONTENTS

A NOTE ON THE TEXT

THIS BOOK USES THE ORIGINAL North American Super Nintendo (SNES) release of *Final Fantasy VI* (1994) as translated by Ted Woolsey as its basis: Unless noted otherwise, all names and dialogue are drawn from that version. Players may remember this version released as *Final Fantasy III*: It was titled so because it was the third installment of the series to be released in North America, having followed the first *Final Fantasy* (1987) on the Nintendo Entertainment System (NES), and *Final Fantasy IV* as *Final Fantasy II* (1991) on the SNES. In the present, the Final Fantasy series restores the games to their original Japanese titles so as to preserve their true order in the main series.

As you read along and encounter mentions of music both from *FF6* and from the worlds of popular and classical music, you may wish to look up those pieces of music online and have a listen. Legal versions of copyrighted music are currently widely available on both Spotify and Apple Music.

PRELUDE

POP IN THE CARTRIDGE FOR *Final Fantasy*, push the power button on your NES, and the screen goes blue: You hear the beginning of an echoing arpeggio, a hill-like pattern that climbs up one harmony and tumbles back down— the first pip of the game's prelude. Words emerge from the void: "The world is veiled in darkness. The wind stops, the sea is wild, and the earth begins to rot. The people wait, their only hope, a prophecy..." As the player reads, the arpeggio's body chassés from major to minor harmonies, tiptoeing mistily away from its starting point, then alighting back home. The pattern changes only minimally as it goes, shifting gracefully here and there so each gesture glides into the next. By the time it loops around to the beginning, the prelude has been on a journey. It's objectively the same this second time we hear it, but in our ears, it's changed and grown somehow—as a hero returns, victorious.

This music is a textbook classical prelude. Rote, even. If you look back across the centuries—from Bach to Chopin to Shostakovich—you'll see this is how preludes are built. Take a short-and-sweet scrap of a melody, duplicate it, swap out some harmonies, give it a little twist, duplicate it again, and swap the harmonies again. Lather, rinse, repeat. Whatever happens as you compose, no matter how you choose to resolve, your sturdy kernel of music always sprouts into a whole-sounding piece.

I wrote a prelude a lot like this for my first college music theory class. Mine was a twenty-measure bumper-car accident in the key of A minor. But I wasn't aiming for beauty. I constructed it specifically to complete an assignment. Once I'd plunked my scrap of music into my notation software, I simply manipulated it into a full-length composition based on the parameters set by my professor—repeating the fragment over and over, varying it slightly each time. It was a virtual cut-and-paste job from one harmony to the next, resulting in a boring, mildly satisfying piano piece. A computer could have written it. Mine practically did. That's how easy it is to compose a bad prelude. Still, it took me five days and I turned it in overdue. I got a B plus.

Nobuo Uematsu wrote the prelude for *Final Fantasy* (*FF1*) in under three minutes, as a filler track, to satisfy a last-minute request from the game's director. If he had been in my theory class, it might have gotten completely lost among the work of me and my classmates, like a pearl in a bag of marbles. But Uematsu's prelude is unquestionably a pearl—a masterpiece of simplicity. It brings a lump to the throat of a generation of gamers. It's electronic music whose form reaches back to the Baroque, a musical statement of the FF series's eclecticism: a glossy reimagining of the past colliding head-on with science fiction, a lattice of odd elements crystallizing into something new and unexpected.

The music from *Final Fantasy VI* (1994) sits high in today's large, diverse pantheon of video game soundtracks, and for good reason. It effortlessly quilts disparate styles and genres to create one world from many. It's accessible, quirky, and affecting. The game's iconic opera scene—an unforgettable pinpoint in the timeline of game history— stays with players in a way that few other scenes manage. The game's music regularly tops critics' and fans' picks, ranking above games that have outsold it by a factor of ten or more. Even today, when many games are accompanied by elaborate, filmic scores recorded by live orchestras, it remains a standout. When it comes to music, defining "best" is a fool's errand—but if you were to give it a shot anyway, *FF6* wouldn't be the worst place to start.

Video game music was born in utter humility, as simple aural feedback—arhythmic, amelodic sound cues. Over the years, it has emerged as a diverse, rich medium for musical expression, escaping the bounds of television speakers or crummy headphones tethered to handheld consoles. Game music has moved onto concert stages, has won mainstream music awards, and has carved out a home in our popular consciousness. This trajectory was unfathomable in the mid-80s, into the 90s, and even in the early 00s.

One would think that, after five installments, this motley series of games would either have lost its audience or suffered some destructive creative failure. One would think that, after five soundtracks, Uematsu's energy would have begun to flag, and that his music would shuffle on toward blandness. And yet *Final Fantasy VI* vaults off the backs of its predecessors to strange new heights.

PRIMORDIAL BLOOP

IT STARTED IN THE LATE 50s, with the buzz of an oscillo-scope, the breath of a cooling fan, the clicking of relays. Then came the beeps: simple and spare in the 60s, more common and complicated as the 70s marched on. Usually tuneless and shapeless, usually only indications of what happens on screen: a blip when the dot repre-senting a ping pong ball hits the line representing the paddle, a staticky crash when your triangular spaceship blows up. Rarely would a familiar melody glint from the deep.

Unless you're a John Cage-type, you probably wouldn't consider this music—just stimulus and response. But isn't music noise organized intentionally? That's what those early arcade sounds were, however scant. Not artful, not great, but technically qualified. A Jamaican bobsled team of sound.

But by the early 80s, video game sound—music or static—had begun to glimmer enough to be recog-nized as art. On January 7, 1983, the *Washington Post* published a piece by critic Joseph McLellan, "Pac-Man Overture in G-Whiz"—likely the first-ever published game music criticism. "Play it again, Tron," he starts. "It's an addiction. Music frequently is. And it works subliminally. Music typically does. Of course, the pictures help, too."

He goes on to describe an arcade's soundscape, including those brief fragments of melody, as a genuine musical experience:

> The music mingles with sound effects; sometimes, as in the works of many serious modern composers, it is hard to say where the music begins and the sound effects end. If a fire siren can be music in Varèse's "Ionization," and the sound of cannon can be music in the "1812 Overture," why can't the whoosh of a guided missile or the splat of an enemy being pulverized be music in a video game?

> [...] In a well-stocked and busy game center, the music is semi-aleatory and polytonal: many different musical events happening together, more or less at random. If you listen closely, it sounds like the kind of thing that you have to buy tickets to hear in the haunts of the post-avant-garde.

Drinking in the sounds of an arcade can certainly elicit an emotional or intellectual response, but unlike the music of Varèse and Tchaikovsky, McLellan's arcade sound-world wasn't created with intention, or at least not with the intention of creating a sound-world. Whatever arcade McLellan was in, it's unlikely that the owner or manager arranged the games to create a sonic experience; the machines were probably placed strategically to impel folks to pump quarters in until their thumbs turned to ash. Arcade cabinets, so arranged, making their discrete sets of sounds, are not an orchestra; they're a raucous bunch of solo acts busking for change.

When I listen to music, I seek out catchy rhythm, regular meter, memorable melodies, and digestible harmonies. Some pieces can be challenging to listen to because they omit one or more (or all) of these listener-friendly qualities. Think the bubblegum easiness of the Beatles' "I Want to Hold Your Hand" against the abstractness, tunelessness, even unpleasantness of "Revolution 9"—which was inspired in part by John Cage, according to Paul McCartney. I've been trained or encultured to look for the familiar signposts in the former—you probably look for them too—which is why I find the latter a little baffling. I love plenty of music that requires some investigation, but the further it strays from the familiar, the easier it is for me to lose the trail. Music can provide clues for us listeners—that's why we can sometimes predict where a song is going before it gets there, even if we've never heard it before. We follow the music's trail, we dust for the artist's fingerprints, and, when the song winds to a finish, the case is closed. That feeling of solving is the song's resolution—it's one of the things that can make listening pleasurable. It's one way you might differentiate "music" from "soundscape."

If this is how we define true music—not just as organized noise, but as sound with clear and carefully placed signposts, designed to effect an emotional or intellectual response—then music began its slow creep into video games toward the end of the 70s and into the early 80s, both at the arcade and in living rooms. Some of it is what McLellan is describing: simple, single-track ditties, usually only a few seconds long, and usually not very satisfying to listen to—but music all the same. Maybe it was the first few notes of Bach's "Toccata and Fugue in D minor," as in *Zarzon* (1981) or *Donkey Kong Jr.* (1982); or Mozart's *Eine kleine Nachtmusik*, as in *Mario Bros.* (1983). (Even if the names of these pieces aren't familiar, I bet you'd recognize them if you heard them.) These melodies usually played only at the start of the game or the beginning or end of a level, then melted away into the arcade-scape.

The gradual move of video game music from disorganization to organization mirrors, in micro, the development of music from prehistory to the modern era. From the lost sounds of early human vocalizations, to ancient percussion and bone flutes, to lutes and lyres, to orchestras and boy bands—thirty or forty millennia. From the static of the first CRT to *Super Mario Bros.* to the studio-recorded tracks of modern video games, thirty or forty years.

To simplify a complicated, subjective history of music: Western music, with its most familiar-to-us signposts, began to take form during the Renaissance. To me, earlier music sounds slightly misshapen—not ugly, sometimes quite lovely, but usually a little alien. Like Medieval manuscript illuminations, early music can be stunningly ornate—but bless those monks, they just couldn't figure out how to draw faces. The sea change in Western music's sound roughly coincides with the introduction of the printing press to Europe—around 1440. The first sheet music printed with movable type cropped up a few decades later—and gradually, printed music and music-related texts became easier to disseminate. That dissemination of ideas helped to homogenize and advance, over time, the sound of European music. Music from the Renaissance is still popular today: It's regularly performed in churches, by professional ensembles, and by high-school choirs. Some musical forms that sprang up during the Renaissance, such as the madrigal, are still being used in modern compositions.

The Gutenberg press of video game music was the Famicom, released in Japan in July 1983, then in the

US as the Nintendo Entertainment System (NES) in October 1985. It was a hugely popular console—it ultimately sold over 60 million units around the world—and helped the video game industry recover from its 1983 crash. Games once again could be distributed and played widely, like those scores printed with movable type. It was accessible, meaning the console and its games were relatively affordable and easy to find, unlike many home computers. Most importantly, these affordable machines had powerful audio hardware—matching, sometimes exceeding, the capabilities of expensive home computers—that allowed composers to level up their work.

The NES has two square wave channels and one triangle wave channel, meaning it can play three tones at once—just enough to create clear harmonic progressions. It also has a generator for "noise," typically used to emulate percussion or create sound effects complementing onscreen action. As a bonus—cartridge space permitting—it has a fifth channel for recorded sound samples.

The earliest NES games sound much like their arcade and home console predecessors: little tunes that play under the start screen, bookend levels, or help you mourn a game over. The non-super Mario Bros. works exactly this way. *Excitebike* (1985) has a toe-tapping opening number, slightly more tense music for its level-select screen, and a cheerful end-of-race fanfare when you place first—but otherwise uses the console's sound channels to mimic motorcycle noise. *Duck Hunt* (1984), in addition to the usual title/game-start/game-over music, uses a two-second jingle when your hound picks up a dead duck. In the rare case that music played throughout gameplay, it was usually monophonic—a single tone with no harmony—and in a lower register. You can hear this kind of background music in *Kung Fu* (1985) and *Donkey Kong* (1986). A short bassline—rarely exceeding ten seconds in length—thrums underneath the sound effects.

It wasn't until about two years after the Famicom's release that composers started taking fuller advantage of its sound hardware. Several games published in the summer of 1985, shortly before the NES reached the US, had truly satisfying scores—among them, the iconic *Super Mario Bros.*, which hit shelves in Japan that September. In his book about the game's music, Andrew Schartmann writes: "[M]usical success in the video-game industry requires a complete product—one that provides quality and innovation in all facets of the gaming experience." That is, one reason the music of *Super Mario Bros.* is so iconic is because it was packaged with an extraordinary game. But that's not the only reason—the music itself is interesting enough not to be off-putting when it's repeated over and over. It's smart, catchy, and playful. It's a far cry from its primitive arcade forebears. It's "real" music that engages melody, harmony, meter, and rhythm in a truly satisfying way. Its overworld theme begins with an instantly identifiable, compelling riff—up there with the opening motif from Beethoven's *Symphony no. 5* as one of the most widely recognizable fragments in the history of music.

In the US in the 80s and 90s, video games were marketed as children's toys. This hobbled the medium for decades, making it difficult to consider it a legitimate means of artistic expression. Scaremongering journalism linked video games to violent behavior, social maladjustment, addiction, and other societal ills (a link that is still regularly unearthed and rehashed). The idea that video games were for kids and teens only—and that game-playing teens would grow up to destroy society—was naggingly persistent until the first crop of gamer kids, mostly born in the 70s and 80s, grew into well-adjusted adults. Grown-up Generation-Xers and Millennials have found we still like video games and have changed the conversation surrounding them, or the medium grew up alongside us and the conversation changed naturally, or both.

Ideas about video game music changed, too. We Gen-Xers and Millennials who grew into game-loving adults carried our familiar childhood game music with us. In many cases, our earliest experiences with video games had also been some of our earliest experiences with music. But to many, that music was still invisible, fully tethered to the game experience—hummable background noise. When would game music cross that vague, ineffable cultural threshold required for us to recognize it as art? At what point would 8- or 16-bit music leap out of the cartridge, out of the living room? How would it end up where it is now—on concert stages, on streaming services, in viral videos, even played at weddings?

The story begins with two little Japanese role-playing video games.

•

Dragon Quest (1986) was a milestone for video role-playing games. It welcomed newcomers to the genre by simplifying the mechanics of tabletop and early computer RPGs. It did away with job classes and fantasy races, pared down character stats to a select few, and limited the party to a single character. Though it retained turn-based combat, it did away with the strategic, tabletop-like movement of avatars through a battlefield—instead, battle screens showed an unmoving, head-on view of a single enemy. To help players feel a sense of progress, it maintained experience points, leveling up and stat increases, and weapon-and-armor upgrades. It capitalized on the open-world, top-down design that made The *Legend of Zelda* (1987) such a hit, but it added a scripted story that Zelda lacked, as well as greater interactivity between player and non-player characters—brand-new elements to NES games.

Despite its innovation, *Dragon Quest* (*DQ1*) was an off-the-shelf knights-and-swords affair. Your chunky little avatar rescues a princess, slays the evil Dragon Lord, and restores peace to the world. Its simple graphics, threadbare plot, and stark music make for a pretty dry game. A plain tortilla chip: One can certainly take simple pleasure in crunching into it—sweet corn and salt and oil—but later games have been flavor-blasted with cool ranch or habanero cheddar. Its relative flavorlessness did not hold it back, though: *DQ1* was a hit in Japan, and it sold more than two million copies. It was an unfortunate commercial flop in the US (released in 1989 and retitled *Dragon Warrior*), but plenty of folks still played it: *Nintendo Power* magazine gave about a million free copies away to new subscribers.

But its true success isn't in its sales or distribution; it's in its legacy. *DQ1* became an archetype for an entire genre—the Japanese role-playing game, or JRPG. JRPGs were slowly distinguishing themselves from Western RPGs by focusing on strictly enforced narratives, more cartoonish graphics, and (typically) simpler mechanics. The JRPG exploded in popularity in the decade that followed, eclipsing its Western counterpart to dominate 90s console RPGs.

DQ1 was also an important advancement for video game music: composer Koichi Sugiyama's work added sophistication, and an impressive pedigree, to the industry's small but growing library of scores. Sugiyama is the world's oldest game composer, born in 1931—28 years before Nobuo Uematsu. His career began before the advent of arcade games, let alone the Famicom. Before *DQ1*, he had a distinguished oeuvre under his belt, having written decades of songs for pop singers, television shows, commercials, movies, and musicals. His music began to appear on TV in the 60s, years before Uematsu began experimenting with music for the first time.

Despite their age difference, Sugiyama and Uematsu entered the video game world at roughly the same time. *DQ1*, with Sugiyama at the 8-bit podium, was released in May 1986—a month after Uematsu's debut work on the PC-88 sci-fi computer RPG *Cruise Chaser Blassty*. Sugiyama has continued his work on the Dragon Quest series ever since, and he became so wrapped up in the franchise that it has come to define his career—much as Uematsu's is defined by Final Fantasy.

•

Nobuo Uematsu wears glasses and a scruffy mustache; these days, his wiry salt-and-pepper hair is usually pulled back in a ponytail and sometimes dressed with a jaunty handkerchief. He loves the Beatles and Led Zeppelin. The first record he ever owned was Elton John's *Honky Château*. He brews his own ale and is confident he has seen ghosts. He embraces and lives his dad-rock truth: In 2002, in his 40s, he formed a prog rock group called the Black Mages, which played covers of the music he composed for the Final Fantasy series—as close to a garage band as a man of his stature could possibly get.

But he's no quirky mediocre weekend rocker. Uematsu's garage band is a beloved side project to a dazzling international musical career. He has enthusiastic fans all over the world, and he's popular in a way few living composers can manage. Orchestras scramble to program his music to cash in on his cachet. When he appears at concerts, crowds thunder for him in a way some symphony halls may not have heard in decades. As early as September 1994, just before *FF6*'s US release, *Diehard GameFan* magazine described him as "godlike."

Uematsu is no god, but instead a liminal composer, existing between musical borders rather than across them. He is and is not a maestro; he composes for and conducts orchestras but is a non-entity in the insular classical music world. The majority of his work is heard but not performed; his instruments are immaterial, and his musicians are millions of tiny grey or black boxes crammed somewhere near a television. His compositional style is both and neither classical and/nor contemporary. His music is popular, but it isn't pop music. His work is, by some measures, derivative and easy to classify; by others, he both defies and defines a genre.

Uematsu's music is familiar as much as it isn't, and that's its defining feature. It sounds like something that should already have existed. It calls attention to itself and diverts attention from itself; it's both assertive and self-effacing. So what does it sound like? What style is it? How is it written?

When I asked him in an email exchange to describe his composition style, he responded simply: "It's like talking to a friend."

When Nobuo Uematsu scored his first video game in 1986, he was not expecting to make a dent in music history. He didn't even expect his first gig at Square (formally Square, Co., Ltd.) to become a regular thing, much less materialize into a career. "Game music didn't exist as a job back then as far as most people knew," he told the Red Bull Music Academy Daily in 2014. "I thought I'd just do game music for a couple of years and then move on to something […] like film music, or writing popular music."

Uematsu was born in 1959 in Kōchi, Japan (today, less populous than Tulsa, Oklahoma). While he enjoyed music from an early age, he never studied it formally. He taught himself to play guitar and piano by ear, at the relatively late, post-prodigy age of eleven or twelve. As a teenager, he wrote for and played in a rock band with friends from school, but his parents wouldn't permit him to study music in college. Still, he knew he wanted to make a career of it.

After he finished college in 1981, he was desperate to break into the music industry—a tall order for someone with no connections and no formal training. He sent out demo tapes indiscriminately, day after day; if he couldn't be the most talented or the best connected, he reasoned, he would at least be the most persistent. He skipped meals to make ends meet, and he took any work that came his way. One of his first music gigs was for Nikkatsu Roman Porno, a series of softcore porn flicks for which he wrote and recorded 50 tracks in just a couple of days. "I can't be proud of it," he told me. The pace was so grueling that he focused on quantity over quality. "That was my job, not my work."

Uematsu lived alone in a studio apartment in Tokyo. Every night, he would have friends and neighbors over for drinks—bohemian types, mostly aspiring artists and writers. One of them, Miki Yukinoura, happened to be working on a video game—*Cruise Chaser Blassty*—and asked Uematsu if he might be interested in helping out with the music. Video game music was a far cry from the film scores and pop songs Uematsu dreamed of writing. This was not supposed to be a big break. Scoring games in the 80s was just about as thankless as scoring soundtracks for VHS porn. Folks weren't playing either for the music.

But he took the gig, helping arrange *Blassty*'s music for synthesizers. His work with Square might have ended after this single project, but fate intervened: One of the game's designers was Hironobu Sakaguchi, who would later go on to design, write, produce, and/or direct the first eleven core installments in the Final Fantasy series. When Square spun off from its parent company in September 1986, Sakaguchi became the new entity's director of planning and development. He offered Uematsu a full-time job.

•

Uematsu is so often compared to the likes of John Williams or Beethoven—both of whom have expansive, revered bodies of work—and is even sometimes called "The Beethoven of Video Game Music." I think this is a bit facile—poor Ludwig is used as a point of comparison so often that anyone who's good at anything may as well be the Beethoven of that thing: Stan Lee was the Beethoven of comic-writing; Albert Einstein was the Beethoven of chalkboards, relativity, and cool hair; Vanna White is the Beethoven of knowing where letters are. Uematsu and Beethoven really have little in common beyond their immense popularity and the number nine—Uematsu's nine Final Fantasy games; Beethoven's nine symphonies.

Maybe "The Puccini of Video Game Music" is more apt. Puccini's claim to fame is a modest body of operas; *La Bohème*, *Tosca*, and *Madame Butterfly* are the most famous of his compositions. Though he wrote other pieces to be performed off the operatic stage, most folks—even classical music fans—would be hard pressed to name any. Both Puccini and Uematsu draw on varied traditions to achieve particular dramatic effects. Both craft imminently singable melodies and smartly use familiar harmonies to tug at the heartstrings. Both of them have proven especially good at writing music for women—Puccini's Mimì and Tosca and Cio-Cio-san; Uematsu's Rosa and Celes and Aerith. Like Puccini, Uematsu's music could justifiably be criticized for simplicity. And, like Puccini, Uematsu has outstripped almost all of his contemporaries in popularity. His name and his work have been canonized.

I love Uematsu's music and don't think of it as overly simple, but I wouldn't describe his writing as technically stunning, either. His music, at least in the 8- and 16-bit eras, mostly avoids virtuosity—it's relatively easy to sing or play. It forgoes flashy and settles for sturdy. It exploits commonly understood musical ideas as a kind of shorthand, but manages this without feeling derivative. This simplicity is due partly to technological limits, which restricted his music's form and texture. It may also be that 20th-century video games were largely marketed as toys for kids and young teenagers, so he accommodated his intended audience with music that was accessible without being condescending.

Another factor in his music's simplicity: It's hard to push the borders of a given medium when you have to map them out for yourself. When Uematsu began working at Square, the practice of scoring video games with constant background music was still new. By the time he really began to brush at the fringes of the NES hardware's capabilities with sophisticated sequencing techniques—as he did in some tracks for *Final Fantasy III* (Famicom, 1990)—the NES had become outmoded by the Super Nintendo (SNES). When he began to hit the SNES's limits with *FF6*, it was time to move on to the PlayStation and *FF7* (1997).

The technological limitations he faced, especially on the NES, may have actually worked in his favor—in spite of the strict limits they put on his sound. "I think that the more limited people are, the more ingenious they begin to get," he told the Red Bull Music Academy Daily, "so maybe I actually enjoyed thinking about how I could make rock music with three sounds, or how I could make classical-sounding music. It was like a game to me." Uematsu isn't the only musician to prosper in this kind of environment. Influential musicians of all types and eras have MacGyvered their way through their work—taking just a Swiss Army knife, some duct tape, and a paperclip to create something magical.

Mozart, for example, found breaches in the strict musical bounds of the Classical period and exploited them to create charming, groundbreaking music. He pushed the nascent concerto form to new limits, and he was shrewd in adopting the clarinet and the piano—new musical technology at the time—to give his music a forward-looking sound. He steeped his work with emotional meaning in a way earlier composers and his contemporaries hadn't and weren't. In an era with rigid expectations about the way music was structured and the way the harmonies worked together, Mozart soared: He composed more than 600 works—including more than 40 symphonies and more than 20 operas—and steered the course of music history. He was only 35 when he died.

Jumping ahead a few hundred years: The garage-rock duo The White Stripes also worked under a set of extreme—in this case self-imposed—musical boundaries. Bandmates Jack and Meg White's approach to producing and performing was highly idiosyncratic: a tightly controlled visual brand; limited studio time to record albums; playing on battered old instruments; and performing without written setlists. As Jack explains in the 2009 documentary *Under Great White Northern Lights*:

> A big component of The White Stripes [is]
> constriction to force ourselves to create.
> Only having red, white, and black colors
> on any of our artwork, our presentation, the
> aesthetics of the band; guitar, drums, and
> vocals; storytelling, melody, and rhythm—
> revolving all these things around the num-
> ber three. All these things force us to create.

The White Stripes were limited to just three voices—Jack's, Meg's, a guitar or other solo instrument—and some percussion. (Four channels in total—just like the NES.) Their intentionally primitive sound helped them generate electric live performances, earn wide commercial success, and produce award-winning albums.

"The more constraints one imposes, the more one frees one's self," wrote Igor Stravinsky in his book *Poetics of Music*. "And the arbitrariness of the constraint serves only to obtain precision of execution."

It may well be that the limits of the NES's audio hardware are the reason Uematsu's music from *Final Fantasy* is uncannily durable. As Mozart was by the musical mores of the Classical era, Uematsu was restricted in form by the nature of NES games—songs were limited in duration, had to repeat. And as The White Stripes chose to be, he was limited to a specific variety and number of instruments. Uematsu excelled nonetheless, and composed several tracks that have been rearranged, borrowed from, and reused in nearly every subsequent title in the series—the driving bassline from the very first battle theme; the victory fanfare, heard when the player has won a battle; and the series's main anthem, first appearing toward the beginning of the game, when the heroes cross a bridge into the great unknown. And, of course, our beloved prelude.

Just as Uematsu taught himself the guitar and the piano, he taught himself to compose for the Famicom. Who was around to teach him? In his early days at Square, he wasn't in contact with Koichi Sugiyama, though as his career advanced he would receive advice from his elder. Few composers were working on, let alone masters of, the Famicom's hardware. Still, he successfully stumbled his way through *FF1*, producing a soundtrack sturdy enough to support the rest of the series.

•

Dragon Quest games hew close to Arthurian-style fantasy, but in Final Fantasy, fantasy-based vampires, werewolves, and unicorns exist alongside reality-based ninjas, pirates, and ankylosaurs. Global cultural and mythological elements are blended together with such nonchalance that you might not even realize it's happening. Chimeras and Medusas are borrowed from Greek mythology, golems from Jewish folklore, manticores from Persian legend—you get the idea. This great potpourri of the fantastic and mythological is salted with science fiction and finished off with a dash of reality: When you're not beating back nagas, gargoyles, and robots, you're squashing spiders, cobras, and lobsters. This is the DNA of the FF series: fantasy in drag as science fiction, ancient cosplaying as contemporary, fantastic and familiar all at once.

Nobuo Uematsu's music does something similar. Where his DQ counterparts stick closer to a classical-inspired sound, Uematsu wanders. He cites prog rock, ABBA, Tchaikovsky, Elton John, Celtic folk, and Keith Urban as influences. He crashes through styles from around the world with abandon, switching lanes from one piece to the next, sometimes driving in two lanes at once, and sometimes going backward. His eclecticism is evident from the series's first installment: On one hand, there are the prelude and the stately anthem that have come to define the series's soundtracks; on the other, there are rock-and-roll battles, funk-influenced dungeons, and a slightly surreal space station. It's "liminal" rendered in song.

American audiences were hungry for something only *FF1* was serving—the series's wild succotash of genres and cultures and realities, both in story and in music. We are a nation of subcultures coexisting, conflicting, coopted, and reclaimed. In a way, *FF1* satisfies the ideal, and reflects the reality, of the American melting pot: for better, a smooth amalgamation of the *pluribus* into one beautifully weird *unum*; for worse, a kind of colonization that appropriates, decontextualizes, and ultimately erases the uniqueness of the cultures and traditions it "borrows" from.

This may explain how, for American audiences at least, Uematsu's music seemed to eclipse Sugiyama's work on the DQ series. It isn't quite apples-to-apples, but let's compare the first two entries in each series. *FF1* outdoes its counterpart in girth, complexity, range, and—though it's subjective—enjoyability. *DQ1*'s score comprises eight unique pieces of music, mostly sticks to two voices, and is overall pretty somber. Fanfare-anthems bookend the game, and cheerful music plays in villages—but the player spends an overwhelming majority of time listening to tense or windburned music, as in the battles, dungeons, and overworld. *FF1*, on the other hand, crosses the finish line with nineteen unique pieces of music, pretty consistently uses all three tone-channels, and takes the listener all over the emotional map: cheerfulness, anxiety, excitement, depression, and resolve.

Uematsu would never admit that his *FF1* soundtrack outshone Sugiyama's *DQ1*—indeed, all of Dragon Quest's NES installments—or maybe he doesn't believe it. Either way, there are small points at which his work defers, ever so slightly, to Sugiyama. In *Final Fantasy II*

(1988) and *Final Fantasy III* (1990), for example, he seems to nod toward *DQ1*'s overworld theme (figure 2.1). *FF2*'s overworld theme (figure 2.2) sticks to two voices, as Sugiyama's did in *DQ1*; they also have the same texture—a smooth melody over an arpeggiated bassline. *FF2*'s "Ancient Castle" (figure 2.3) quotes *DQ1*'s overworld theme almost note for note, as does *FF3*'s "The Crystal Tower" (figure 2.4). These are small gestures—possibly accidental—but feel like a short bow, a show of reverence. Or imitation—that paragon of flattery.

Figure 2.1 Overworld Theme from Dragon Quest, *mm. 1–5.*

Figure 2.2 Overworld Theme from Final Fantasy
II, *mm. 1–4. Note the similarity in texture here to
the overworld theme from* Dragon Quest: *a lonely,
continuous melody accompanied by an arpeggiated
eighth-note pattern.*

Figure 2.3 "Ancient Castle" from Final Fantasy II, *mm. 1–5 (bassline omitted). Note how the circled notes in this excerpt roughly (sometimes exactly) mimic the melodic outline of the overworld theme from* Dragon Quest. *Like both games' overworld themes, it is accompanied by a similar eighth-note pattern.*

Figure 2.4 "The Crystal Tower" from Final Fantasy III, *mm. 1–9 (bassline omitted). As with figure 2.3, this piece mimics* Dragon Quest's *overworld theme, both in its melody and in the second voice's arpeggios. In this case, the similarity is even more striking, and includes more of Sugiyama's original material.*

"It's probably just a coincidence," he tells me in an email. "Just being compared to Sugiyama-*sensei* is humbling." As a listener, though, I can't help but think the similarities in these pieces, and others, betrays his true regard—the musical connection between the two men sounds clear. Uematsu's admiration for Sugiyama shines directly through his work.

•

In the 8- and 16-bit eras, Uematsu's style feels distinctive. In addition to his eclecticism, he has a panache for melody and a welcoming approach to his writing. Just as the game's developers sought to emulate *DQ1* but differentiate *FF1* from it, Sakaguchi wanted Uematsu to create a different kind of sound.

Uematsu recalled his beginnings at Square in a 1999 interview: "At the time, I didn't know what game music was." So before he wrote a note, Sakaguchi instructed the composer to play *DQ1*. Sugiyama's classically refined style formed a framework for Uematsu's ideas of game music—but to create a different sound, as Sakaguchi desired, Uematsu took his own approach to composition. He created his pieces' melodies first, then went back and "orchestrated" them. At the time, he was working on the Famicom, so "orchestration" meant adding the texture and harmonies the console was capable of. "I struggled to produce originality in the same three tones," he said in another interview later that year. "I had to focus on the melody itself and think about how each chord would move the audience."

His contemporaries, Koichi Sugiyama and Koji Kondo—the latter of whom was responsible for the music from the Mario and Zelda series—must certainly have thought about how each compositional move they made would affect their audience as well. So how is Uematsu's music different, especially from Sugiyama's? Perhaps because of his influences and listening habits, and likely in part because of his lack of formal training, he seems to have been less inhibited in his writing, inclined to produce melodies that were easy to understand and easy to sing, and harmonies that wouldn't be out of place in pop vernacular.

Koji Kondo's harmonies are easy to understand, and his melodies are memorable enough. But his tunes aren't exactly easy to sing: The overworld themes from Zelda and Mario both span over an octave and a half—a range as virtuosic as an opera aria—and the theme from Mario closes in on two full octaves. Sugiyama, meanwhile, writes intelligent, well-executed music—but his harmonies can be crunchy, and sometimes his melodies get lost in the shuffle. Think of the battle themes from the first few entries in the DQ series; they're effectively tense, but there's little to hum in the shower. Uematsu, however, nails both singable melody and digestible harmony in so much of his music, making it easier to carry with you once you set the controller down. This reflects something fundamental in the way he thinks about music. "There's rhythm and there's melody," he says in a 1994 interview. "Rhythm only reaches the body [...] melodies, however, do reach one's soul."

As Uematsu's choice of instruments expanded in the 16-bit era, his Sugiyama-influenced classical framework became a little more apparent. So did his exploration of genre—it's here that he begins to fully realize the prismatic sound the Final Fantasy series begs for, and where he truly differentiates his sound from Sugiyama's. Games that so casually blend the unblendable should have music that does the same—and in the 16-bit era, Uematsu served this more plainly than ever.

"I love progressive rock," he said in a 2011 interview, "[b]ecause you [can] put any genre of music into it." Indeed, prog rock's influence on his work is sometimes baldly apparent. Compare, for example, Boston's "Foreplay / Long Time" (1976) to *FF5*'s "Battle at the Big Bridge" and *FF6*'s "Dancing Mad." Or try comparing "Dancing Mad" to the three-movement, organ-heavy "Three Fates" (1970) by Emerson, Lake & Palmer. Tchaikovsky's influence is less explicit. Certain musical moments in Final Fantasy do recall his Romantic-era sensibilities: The last section in *FF6*'s "Cyan" resembles the love theme from *Romeo and Juliet* (see figures 2.5 and 2.6). But I think the Romantic influence is more in compositional approach rather than outright similarity in sound: Tchaikovsky's work is recognized for its memorable melodies, easy harmonies, and panache for pastiche—three areas in which Uematsu shines.

Figure 2.5 "Cyan" from Final Fantasy VI, *mm. 13–14 (strings, melody only).*

Figure 2.6 Tchaikovsky, "Love Theme" from Romeo and Juliet, *mm. 212–215 (oboe). As with the quoted material from "Cyan" in figure 2.4, this familiar passage begins with an upward half-step, leaps down a bit further, then, after a quick wave-like motion, resolves back up. Both fragments end a major third lower than they began—they both have the same destination, even if they take different routes.*

Uematsu's pastiche encompasses more than rock and classical. He burgles from everywhere. No genre is safe. As a case study: Every FF game from *FF2* onward incorporates his Chocobo theme—which accompanies characters as they ride giant land-birds, a cross between an ostrich and a marshmallow Peep. Almost every recurrence of the theme is plunked into a new genre: samba, bluegrass, techno, mambo, chiptune, surf rock, mod, and Dave Brubeck-like quintuple meter. In his 16-bit games alone, he invokes sea shanties; Scandinavian, Celtic, and East Asian folk music; ragtime; West African drumming; industrial; rockabilly; and Viennese waltz.

Uematsu is a musical polyglot, switching genres as needed to best suit a given situation to speak to a broad audience. Unlikely hodgepodge is a key component of the Final Fantasy series—and Uematsu's soundtracks pull it off just as casually as the games themselves. Again, this is his signature: "Talking to a friend." Taking ideas from diverse sources and translating them into a language any of one of us—any of his dear friends—can understand.

•

Final Fantasy music has slowly wandered its way out of the cartridge and off of the game disc. Printed music scores have been released commercially—for solo piano, for live orchestra, for rock groups, even for a cappella ensemble. Recordings have been published as well—some ripped straight from the games, others performed by piano soloists, orchestras, cover bands, and more. Live performances of FF music have taken symphony halls by storm. Forged from a slim set of square and triangle waves, Uematsu's music has helped game music become the phenomenon—the genre—as we now know it. His music is made for this kind of treatment—it begs for it. It steals from everywhere, and we, the public, are Robin Hood: justly redistributing to genres, platforms, and stages as we see fit.

Is it Uematsu alone who propelled game music into the popular consciousness? Probably not. Could it have happened without him? It's impossible to say, but my money is on no. It's hard to trace who did what to get us to where we are today. The lines of music history crisscross and double back; they spiral and double and shoot forward. All we can say for certain is that, at some point, game music wasn't. And now it is.

Like a classical prelude, it starts small: the whir of an oscilloscope, the crash of a spaceship, the beep of ping-pong paddle. An unspoken wish for music. "The people wait, their only hope, a prophecy…"

These are the heroes foretold in legend: our lost sounds, our bone flutes, our lyres and lutes. From an unspoken wish for music, from an 80s soundscape, a pip is formed. It journeys from bit to bit, system to system, arcade cabinet to cartridge to disc. It grows almost imperceptibly on each step of the adventure. Eventually it returns home, to a wish fulfilled. These unlikely heroes have emerged from the primordial bloop, forging ahead into the world of rhythm and melody, leveling up, and fighting that big boss—cultural gatekeepers—to change the course of music history. From the clicking of relays to a blue screen and a prophecy. From three minutes and an arpeggio to bands, orchestras, screens, stereos, and stages around the world.

THE ZEROTH HALF

FINAL FANTASY VI's PLOT is a tangled-up Slinky. For a newcomer to understand what's going on, several separate, complicated stories need describing—and none is complete without the others. This is gonna get messy.

I see the game as split into three halves. The zeroth half is a tremendous amount of backstory: Character development for its fourteen heroes starts offscreen, before the player enters the game—you catch up on it in flashbacks, or scraps of dialogue, as you go. The backstory is as important as the frontstory, and there is enough of it to fill its own decent—but disjointed—game.

The first true half of the game begins the instant the player takes control—it is set in what the official player's guide calls the World of Balance, where a mostly linear plot unfolds. There is a brief scene on the Floating Continent, which ends with the game's biggest twist: the apocalypse. As the second half of the game begins, the World of Balance turns into the World of Ruin, and the linear plot turns into a set of mostly optional, mostly unrelated side quests. Once the player completes the few required objectives in the World of Ruin, they can choose to face the game's final villain whenever they like—but the more optional side quests they complete, the more powerful their characters become, and the easier it is to beat the game.

•

The following text overlays the game's introduction:

> Long ago, the War of the Magi reduced the world to a scorched wasteland, and magic simply ceased to exist. 1000 years have passed… Iron, gunpowder, and steam engines have been rediscovered, and high technology reigns… But there are some who would enslave the world by reviving the dread destructive force known as "magic." Can it be that those in power are on the verge of repeating a senseless and deadly mistake?

None of this is inaccurate, but it leaves out just about all of the details the player needs to make sense of the game. The real exposition has been chopped up and sprinkled throughout the script, coming to the player in bits and pieces, usually just—but not always—in time for the player to really understand what's happening on screen.

In the World of Balance, about two decades before the game begins, a political force known as the Empire—headed by Emperor Gestahl and his flunky clown-mage, Kefka—gained tremendous power. Gestahl was interested in acquiring and weaponizing magic power so his empire could crush, conquer, and rule the world. To do this, he located the portal to the world of the Espers, the race of beings at the heart of the War of the Magi, who had withdrawn from the human world to stop the bloodshed once and for all. Gestahl and Kefka, flanked by storm troopers, cracked open the portal and kidnapped a small number of Espers; the remaining Espers magically expelled the humans and sealed the portal again, this time for good. In kicking the humans to the curb, however, they also lost two of their own. Madonna, the only human known to be friendly with their people, had wandered by mistake into their world years before, fallen in love with an Esper named Maduin, and borne a child named Terra—half-human, half-Esper. Mother and daughter were whisked back to the human realm, where Emperor Gestahl murdered the mother and snatched the baby. Terra was raised as an Imperial slave.

The kidnapped Espers were taken to the Imperial capital, Vector, and placed in a laboratory that researched how to extract their magical power and transfer it to human beings. Kefka, the Emperor's right hand, was the first human to be experimented on. He successfully gained magical powers but suffered brain damage, became mentally unstable, and turned into a mad clown, Joker-style. Still, his power made him a valuable asset to the Emperor, who kept him around as a court mage and lackey. When the magic infusions were fully refined, others underwent the process: One of them was Celes, who would grow up to become a top Imperial general, and who would eventually denounce the Empire's violence and join in the Returners' resistance effort to take them down.

The game begins two decades later. The Empire is still bent on mining for magical power. They believe Terra is the key: Because of her parentage, her magical power is beyond anything they have so far been able to extract from the captive Espers. They believe she can connect them with her home world, where they might be able to access nearly infinite magical power—but that's their long game. In the meantime, they settle for using her as a weapon as they conquer and occupy nation after nation.

The player enters the game world as Terra, whose mind is controlled through a device called a slave crown. A new Esper, suspended in ice like a caveman in a glacier, has been discovered in the human world, and the Empire has sent Terra to seize it. She is intercepted by an underground resistance movement called the Returners, who free her from slavery. Finally able to act of her own free will, she teams up with the Returners: Locke, a heroic thief; Edgar, a womanizing king; Sabin, a blackbelt and Edgar's twin brother; Cyan, a bereaved knight; Celes, the former Imperial general; Setzer, a wandering gambler, and many others.

Over the first roughly fifteen hours of gameplay, the Returners win victories and suffer setbacks in equal measure, until Kefka and Gestahl finally break through the sealed barrier, track down and slaughter the remaining Espers who escape through the barrier and take refuge in the World of Balance, and at last enter the Esper realm to access a trio of statues—the Goddesses, the source of all magic. In doing so, they rip a continent from the face of the earth. On this Floating Continent, the Returners try one last time to avoid calamity, but they're not strong enough to overcome Gestahl and Kefka's newfound power.

It appears the two are set for world domination—until Kefka shockingly murders his liege and takes the power for himself. He rearranges the petrified Goddesses to his liking, and in doing so, redirects the flow of their magic toward himself. He becomes a godlike being, and his first act post-apotheosis is to send the Floating Continent crashing onto the earth below. The impact destroys the world as the heroes and player know it—and causes an extinction-level event, either killing or mutating the world's flora and fauna. Kefka reigns supreme over the ruins.

The heroes are scattered across the planet, none knowing that the others have survived. Celes, marooned on an island with Cid, rafts her way toward civilization, where she finds the gambler Setzer and the twins Edgar and Sabin. Together, they rove the planet in search of their friends and steel themselves to take on Kefka once and for all.

FF6 went a step further than any other game ever had: Instead of merely flirting with the end of the world, it exchanges vows and says "I do." This game is about the death of a planet, and the seedling of its rebirth. The game could easily, satisfyingly have ended on the Floating Continent, but it goes beyond itself, doubling in length and complexity. Its greatest ambition is that it asks players to reinvest themselves when everything is lost—something the characters must do, too.

•

The plot, with its many other twists and turns, is a reflection of the game's development. The story wasn't written start to finish with a single direction in mind. Rather, the scenario was proposed, then characters were created, their stories were fleshed out, and the scenario was designed to accommodate those stories. *FF6's* director, Yoshinori Kitase, said in a 2013 interview with *Edge* magazine: "We began work on *Final Fantasy VI* with the idea that every character is the protagonist of the story. […] The idea was to transform the [characters] from mere ciphers for fighting into true characters with substance and backstories who could evoke more interesting or complex feelings in the player." At one point, according to producer Hironobu Sakaguchi, there were more than twenty characters developed, but they were combined and narrowed to a more compact fourteen—if that can be considered compact at all.

Everyone on the development team chipped in with their own ideas for characters, which may explain the relatively large cast. To accommodate all of the ideas, the team aimed for a game that allowed characters to develop episodically, rather than trying to manage so many character arcs in a single, uninterrupted narrative. Sprinkled into the main storyline—and into the amorphous storyscape of the World of Ruin—are diversions specifically designed for character development: heartfelt conversations, flashbacks, dream sequences, scavenger hunts, and an opera. Maybe it's inaccurate to say these episodes are "sprinkled in." It might be truer in some cases to say that the game's main quest is sprinkled around these episodes. In the end, it was up to

Kitase to unify all of the game's dramatic elements into a coherent story.

•

There is no music when the world ends. Celes is the only survivor, and she wakes up from a coma on a desert island, accompanied only by waves on the beach. She is alone but for one other person, Cid—an old friend from the Empire, the scientist who infused her with magic, and the man who became the closest thing she had to a father. Cid is gravely ill, and the player, through Celes, is tasked with his care. She must feed him, making trips to the beach to catch fish with her bare hands, bringing them back to her bedridden friend. Depending on how well she does, Cid lives or dies—still no music, only ocean sounds.

This relative lack of music, paradoxically, emphasizes the soundtrack's importance: It builds a world, then has to rebuild it. When everything disappears, that disappearance must be felt in the player's gut—so the music disappears with it. To be so missed, the music must be extraordinary, so wide-ranging and nuanced that it feels like a natural extension of the game's complicated story, characters, and world. Uematsu had to be every bit as ambitious as his colleagues to achieve this. He had to write a soundtrack smart enough, strong enough, and huge enough to bind it all together: Coherency was Uematsu's responsibility just as much as it was Kitase's.

Such a job is not for the faint of heart. Square's *Chrono Trigger* (1995) is often compared with, paired with, or pitted against *FF6* in consideration of 16-bit JRPGs—because of the similarities in their "save the world from inevitable apocalypse" scenarios and their similarly stellar quality. *Chrono Trigger*'s soundtrack was its own herculean undertaking—lots of spaces, events, and characters to define, lots of stories to unify. The game's composer, Yasunori Mitsuda, developed stress-related stomach ulcers toward the game's completion, and required Uematsu's help to cross the finish line.

Despite the tremendous amount of pressure on him during *FF6*'s brisk year-long development, Uematsu was utterly unfazed. When I asked him about it, he said he doesn't recall feeling anxious about this project, nor did he worry about how it would be received. He simply rafted away, confident that he'd reach land on the other side of the horizon. He composed as if unaware that the fate of a world was on his shoulders.

•

FF6's soundtrack spans three compact discs, totals 61 tracks, and clocks in at a little over three hours—massive in comparison to its peers. The two Super Famicom installments of the Dragon Quest series (*DQ5* and *DQ6*) each have less than half as much music on their soundtracks, the soundtrack for *FF5* is only two hours long, and *FF6*'s close sister, *Chrono Trigger*, is two and a half.

Size isn't everything, but it demonstrates Nobuo Uematsu's ambition—and his extraordinary response to his colleagues' ambition—that he outgirthed all his contemporaries and his own previous works. The soundtrack could still have been effective if it had fewer numbers. "Another World of Beasts," for example, could have been cut, and the existing "The Phantom Forest" used in its place. The same goes for "The Fierce Battle" and "The Decisive Battle." In fact, two additional town themes were written for the game but went unused and were omitted from the soundtrack, indicating that Uematsu already did some such economizing—and there are other places he could possibly have done the same. But going big paid off with a more effective soundtrack, and by consequence a game with more precisely formed settings and characters.

Uematsu also took artistic and technical risks he had never done before—some that no one ever had. "*Final Fantasy VI* was actually the moment I could start experimenting for the first time," he once said. He composed his own little opera, using video game hardware to approximate human song, even though he admitted to me that he had never seen an opera himself. He wrote a wild, prog-rock inspired four-movement suite for the game's final battle—appearing on the soundtrack as a single seventeen-and-a-half-minute track—which advances from one movement to the next based on the player's progress in the fight. He wrote fourteen distinctive character themes, one for each of the heroes (except for the twins, Edgar and Sabin, who share one) and one for the villain Kefka—and he expanded and developed these themes as the game's drama progressed (a compositional approach known—in some contexts, anyway—as "leitmotif"). At several points in the game—the introduction, the opera, and the ending sequence—he times the music to line up precisely with onscreen action, as a film score would.

The soundtrack evokes settings—as the pastoral "Kids Run Through the City" does for peaceful hamlets in the World of Balance, and the somber "The Day After" does for the same towns after they've been ravaged by the apocalypse. It illustrates conflict: in the heart-pounding pieces that play during battles, in the gleeful wickedness of Kefka's theme, in the deep suspicion of Strago's theme, or in the dread of "Catastrophe." And it resolves. Little resolutions, as the victory fanfare that plays after you win a battle, or the morose number that plays when your party dies. Big resolutions, as the final medley that interweaves and wraps up each character's theme and helps put a bow on their stories. The soundtrack—and the game—end with the series's prelude: the ultimate resolution, suggesting a return to peace and balance.

Musicologist Ryan Thompson has suggested that, for numerous reasons, *FF6* is something of an opera itself. He proposes that the game can be split into three acts—broken up differently from my three "halves." It begins, as most operas do, with a prelude/overture—the opening cutscene and first few minutes of gameplay. The first act begins when Terra wakes up after escaping from the Empire, the second begins when Locke wakes up after Terra transforms into her Esper form for the first time, and the third begins when Celes wakes up marooned on that remote island in the World of Ruin. The game's ending sequence serves as a kind of curtain call.

The CD print of the soundtrack seems to intentionally reflect this structure. The music doesn't appear on the discs in its order of appearance in the game, but it does appear in an order that feels dramatically logical. The first disc begins with the music from the opening cutscene—the game's overture—and ends with "Metamorphosis," closely associated with the destructive powers of the Espers; the second disc begins with Terra's character theme and ends with "Another World of Beasts," the music that plays as you approach the Sealed Gate and set in motion the events leading to the apocalypse; the third disc begins with the music from the Floating Continent, where Kefka makes his fateful power grab and sends the world from balance to ruin. The album ends, of course, with music that plays over the end-game sequence. The album, like many operas, is split tidily into three acts.

Characters, narrative, setting, conflict, and resolution: The 61 pieces on *FF6*'s soundtrack play us the game in miniature.

•

On its release, *FF6* received lavish praise from US critics. "Forget every other RPG out there," wrote Danyon Carpenter in October 1994's issue of *Electronic Gaming Monthly*. "[*FF6*] has everything: stunning graphics, incredible music, and so many twists and turns to the plot that you could just play this forever, and heck, why not?" Carpenter's *EGM* colleagues were similarly fervent in their acclaim, hailing it as "epic" and "beautiful" with a liberal use of exclamation points. *GamePro* lauded its graphics as "outstanding," "rich," and imaginative," and its music as "a treat, even for tone-deaf RPG addicts." *Game Informer* asked, "Could this be the perfect RPG?" and then answered by rating it a 9.5 out of 10—not perfect, but the highest score the magazine had ever given at the time of that issue's publication, matched by *Super Metroid* and *Donkey Kong Country* later that same year. (The first RPG to outscore it was *FF7*, which came in at 9.75).

Only *Nintendo Power* seemed to have concrete criticism in addition to the usual praise: They wrote that its story was "not [...] particularly inventive" and "often sappy," that its animation is wanting, and that its cutscenes are overlong. Its numerical "Power Meter Ratings" were good but not excellent: Out of five, it scored 3.9 for graphics and sound, 3.1 for play control, 3.9 for challenge, and 4.0 for theme and fun; if this were a school project, it would have gotten a D—or, on a fair curve with its contemporaries, a B. *FF1* got its own issue of the magazine and *FF4* got a cover spot, but *FF6* got no such star treatment within the pages of the magazine. Players didn't seem to mind: The magazine's "Power Charts" (whose rankings are based on subscriber favorites, voted on by postcard each month) showed *FF6* to be immensely popular. It racked up more than four years in the top 20 list of SNES games—from its release in October 1994 until the magazine stopped tracking votes for SNES games in December 1998.

There has always been some dissent regarding *FF6*'s merit. One can find long forum posts or angry comments decrying the game's supposed overratedness: that its main antagonist is a bland, bargain-bin Joker knockoff; that its protagonists, of which there are far too many, are all one-note; that the story was played out before it was even played. These criticisms aren't based on nothing. The game does have a familiar scenario— the empire-and-rebel setup recalls not just the Star Wars movies but also older Famicom sibling *FF2*. The plot is shaped like a wrung-out sweater, lumpy and amorphous. It's top-loaded with story, which splits, twists, loops, and frays until, in the last half of the game, it disappears completely. The script does its job, but it's no masterwork of writing. The graphics combine several disparate styles: the detailed portrait art in the game's menus is an approximation of Yoshitaka Amano's airy concepts, the character sprites—the avatars the player sees most often—are cartoonishly proportioned, and the battle landscapes lean toward photorealism.

And yet, most critics and fans today continue singing the praises of this decades-old game. On nearly all ranked lists of the Final Fantasy games, *FF6* appears at the top. In June 2017, *Game Informer* ranked it second on its list of the best RPGs of all time. (Its more popular younger brother, *FF7*, ranked a respectable eighteenth.) It won the best-in-series title in RPGFan in April 2011; Kotaku in January 2013; IGN in May 2016; GamesRadar+ in February 2017; Polygon in December 2017; Screen Rant in February 2019; RedBull.com in February 2020; and Digital Trends in early 2020. Kitase—albeit anecdotally—confirms the sentiment, at least for players in Europe and the Americas: "I'm taken aback by the number of westerners who ask me to sign their *Final Fantasy VI* cases," he told *Edge* magazine. "In Japan that would apply more to the subsequent game,

Final Fantasy VII, but I get the impression there's a large number of players in the West who prefer the earlier game."

In one of the world's best-selling video game franchises, it's a clear favorite—even among later installments, with their HD and 4K graphics and live-recorded orchestral music. Uematsu has even said that *FF6* is his favorite. (Note: His answer to this question seems to change with every interview).

This is the little cartridge that could.

In the flurry of opinions about the game, *FF6*'s music remains virtually unimpeached, and is a landmark for modern gamers, critics, and scholars—even those who might have had no formative experience with the game in the 90s, and thus hold some immunity to nostalgia. In a 2015 piece for Kotaku, "What It's Like to Play *Final Fantasy VI* for the First Time," Kirk Hamilton writes: "When I say I haven't played *FFVI*, people usually freak out about the music thing. 'Aren't you a big music guy? Don't you like music? What are you doing!' they cry, flecks of spittle flying from their lips and landing on my glasses. To them I say, well, okay, yes, the music in this game is really good. I love it." New and lifelong fans gush about the music in forums and comment sections, critics write books about it, and music scholars publish papers and present their findings at academic conferences. Other games from the 16-bit era have great soundtracks, too—but few others garner such sustained attention.

Despite its overwhelmingly positive reception, *FF6* was not a runaway commercial success in the US. Sales numbers from the 90s can be hazy, but the title sold between four and five hundred thousand copies in the US in the year following its release. This is a respectable number, to be sure, and higher than the series's earlier titles—but *FF7*'s year-one sales would prove to be about ten times as high. *FF6* is held in such high regard that I'd always assumed its sales were off the charts. It's easy to conflate critical acclaim with commercial success, especially in retrospect. Hironobu Sakaguchi, the game's producer, has expressed surprise that the game is so well-loved in America so long after its release, given its lukewarm sales. In a 2014 interview with Kotaku, he laments: "When I hear you and other fans saying, 'Yeah, *VI* was my favorite!' I'm like, 'Hey, so why didn't you buy it back then?'"

Critical reexamination and scholarly attention are a symptom of the game's endurance, not a cause. *FF6* is not perfect, but I think that's what makes it extraordinary.

I think of Maria Callas—the great soprano, and the likely namesake for the diva the player impersonates in *FF6*'s famous opera. Callas is one of the best-known sopranos of the 20th century, and one of the most iconic figures in opera history. She was highly sought after for her commanding stage presence, her acting, and for her unusually broad repertoire. But her voice was controversial because of its distinctive timbre: To some it sounded raw and unaffected, which made it an emotive powerhouse; to others, it was muddy and unwieldy. Her instrument was pretty, ugly, and sometimes both—but always distinctive. Imperfection is not a color on her palette, but an intrinsic quality. She seems to occupy a liminal space just as Uematsu does: Whatever she is, she is. That liminality, the perfect imperfection of her voice, is why she is still worshipped by so many critics and listeners—even many who discovered opera decades after she passed away.

I fall squarely in the pro-Callas camp. Give me a weird voice over a flawless one any day. From my seat way up in the family circle, where all the faces may as well be eight pixels wide, the weirdest voices are the ones you recognize best. The glossiest ones all sound the same.

•

FF6's characters are rendered with sprites measuring 16 by 24 pixels. The SNES can display 256 of 32,768 colors at a given time. Each character has an unchanging 32-by-32–pixel headshot shown in the game's menu screen, but they appear exclusively in their smaller 16-by-24 form in the rest of the game, during battles and exploration and cutscenes. Each character's sprite has a few dozen variations to show actions such as walking, thinking, casting a spell, fighting, laughing, or gasping in surprise. The combined size and color constraints severely limit the "acting" a character's sprite can do to only the most basic of facial expressions and little body language. Voice acting—while technically possible—was far too impractical to close the gap. Any meaningful use of voice acting would have required more storage than the entirety of the game itself by several orders of magnitude. How is it, then, that we feel like these characters are real? Why do we bond with them and tense up when we think they might kick the bucket?

Welcome to the "Mario Pit"—my rough conceptual mash-up of aesthetic distance and the uncanny valley—the broad canyon between player and pixelated character. In his study on the music of *Super Mario Bros.*, Andrew Schartmann writes:

> Kondo was convinced that game sound could lessen the gap between Mario and the hands that move him. With Kondo's visionary techniques, players do more than control a character on screen; they form an intimate bond with it—a bond forged by the motional spark at the heart of Kondo's music.

The distance between a gamer and a small collection of pixels seems like a pretty big gap to leap across. In some ways, though, this Mario Pit works in the player's favor: The little chunky avatars in *FF6* are detailed enough to resemble cartoon people while avoiding, by a long shot, the uncanny valley's downward dive into pseudo-human creepiness. The uncanny valley describes a low point in an object's trajectory towards human resemblance: Somewhere between the peaks of "cute because it's not so human" and "indistinguishable from a person" is a wide, disturbing gulf, the nadir of which is the 2004 film *The Polar Express*. When games aim for photorealistic characters, our brains fixate on their imperfections, on any hint of alienness. But games like the Mario series, and the 80s and 90s FF titles, provide enough physical detail to convey humanness while avoiding the downhill train-crash of Tom Hanks's most unfortunate cinematic endeavor.

I am far more inclined to empathize with the 80s version of Mario than a lifelike Mario rendered with features that don't quite hit the mark. Think of an ambulatory, costumed, aging wax figure of Lou Albano or Bob Hoskins, both of whom have played live-action versions of Mario—yikes. Now think of an in-game Mario—the cartoonish little guy who lands himself in New Donk City (in *Super Mario Odyssey*, 2017), scuttling around the business-formal, human-proportioned characters. I'm gonna root for the simple cartoon guy over the cadaverous wax figures, thanks and good night.

FF6's characters are drawn *chibi* style, sometimes referred to as "super-deformed," meaning that their heads, torsos, and legs are in equal proportion, similar to Mario's. The choice to depict them this way seems counterintuitive. Kitase himself noted that he wanted the development team to transform the characters from "mere ciphers for fighting" into ones who would "evoke more interesting or complex feelings in the character." One would think that, with limited pixel space, he would have pushed for the characters to appear as human as possible—knowing that, even with the team's best efforts, they could never fall all the way into Ro-bob Hoskins or Lou Al-bot-o territory. Instead, they lean into their technological barriers and create the weird little nuggets we've learned to love. They chose this spot on the curve of the uncanny valley intentionally: the equal head-torso-leg proportion, the large forehead, the chubby arms—these recall the look of infants, beings we are evolutionarily trained to adore. That feeling of adoration, protracted over 40 hours of gameplay, slowly transforms into attachment. Not quite real love—chibi love.

Through this chibi familiarity and the music that enraptures us into it, we hang-glide backward across the uncanny valley, bringing our human selves into *FF6*'s surreal but sympathetic world, jumping across the Mario Pit like a plumber on shrooms.

•

Visuals and interactivity can't necessarily do all the work to make a game great, and neither can a script. Music is an important part of storytelling, scene-setting, and character development in games and a variety of other media. Movies and TV shows are often accompanied by or punctuated with music, and it's the foundation upon which opera and musical theatre are built. In gaming, music complements interactivity, story, and visuals to build a bond between player and character in the same way it does between spectator and character in cinema, television, and theatre.

Our brains respond differently to music than they do to visuals or words. Even simple music can profoundly manipulate our emotions, given the right context. Hear a childhood lullaby for the first time in decades, and it could leave you a blubbering mess. Uematsu isn't our mother singing us to sleep—but he has a razor-sharp instinct for melodic description, and profound understanding of the player-listener's inter-pretation of sound. He knows exactly when the player needs formality, gushiness, cheekiness, or tension—and he seems to know how to evoke any combination of these, in any proportion, based on the situation.

He communicates ideas with less complexity than one might hear in Western classical music, but he doesn't need complexity. For an SNES game, a live-recorded score is just as impossible as truly lifelike representations of humans and their surroundings; it could even widen the Mario Pit, were it mashed up against low-resolution graphics, reminding the player of the distance between the real world and the game world. "We couldn't precisely reproduce instruments," Uematsu told me in an email. "I chose samples that wouldn't lose the original sound's character even if they were 'deformed' to match the rest of the game." Which is to say: Uematsu didn't need the Cleveland Orchestra. He needed the aural equivalent of a 16 by 24–pixel nugget for his portraits, and 256 colors for his landscapes. Nugget music was plenty.

This applies not just to *FF6*'s sound samples, but also to the score itself. The composition possesses its own chibi quality in its bite-size succinctness.

Things began to change in 1997, when *FF7* abandoned the pixel for the polygon. Cloud, Barret, and Tifa move through a semi-3D world with more fluidity than *FF6*'s Terra, Locke, and Edgar manage in their two dimensions. In cutscenes, those polygons can execute movements precise enough to make Aerith's death—as iconic a scene as our game's trip to the opera—surprising and upsetting in a way that it might not have been in the chibi style of *FF6*. *FF7* works more like a film than its older sibling, and Uematsu's music follows suit—it's familiar and smart, but doesn't require the same laser-focused, constant stream of melody. It often drifts into ambient, less-hummable fragments—a smart choice for the game's move toward the cinematic, but a melancholy one. "It's a little sad that *Final Fantasy VI* was the last chibi Final Fantasy game," Uematsu said later in our exchange. "I wish I could have done one or two more with the same atmosphere."

When *FF7* was initially conceived, Uematsu's colleagues thought they would be making another Super Famicom/SNES game. I don't think anyone, Uematsu included, regrets how *FF7* turned out, but I do wonder what kind of chibi magic our guy had left in him, and what melodic marvels we might be singing if he'd had one last encore with his 16-bit orchestra.

NOUN MUSIC

THE PIPE ORGAN IS A LUMBERING, complicated machine of an instrument. It requires your entire body to play and hulks out music through dusty, antique science. Hundreds, thousands, or even hundreds of thousands of delicately assembled mechanical parts bellow a supply of wind through ranks of different-sized pipes. The pipes can produce sounds ranging from monstrously deep to twinkly high, in sometimes hundreds of timbres. Organs can be small and light enough to carry or weigh hundreds of tons and fill up a freight train, but a pipe organ is more than the sum of its many, many parts: It creates a whole world of sound and gives you no choice but to live in it. Like the cathedrals they often inhabit, pipe organs exist in outsize proportion, engineered by humans to evoke the presence of the beyond. Screeching treble and thundering bass conjure the Alpha and Omega; the sound can come from all directions at once, becoming an invisible force that barrels through the bodies of its listeners. Organists sit behind their consoles pressing keys, pulling stops, flipping levers, and stomping on pedals, operating a mech suit that blasts out magic. Music, that most human of endeavors, becomes extrahuman.

At their cores, pipe organs are binary instruments: Their stops are on or off, their sound crescendos and decrescendos accordingly, and they render our input into a primitive kind of digital output. Organs are a triumph of engineering, but they are also an artifact. They have been outmoded in many ways by newer keyboard instruments such as the piano—which, though a complicated machine in itself, responds more organically to the player's input. Pianos have, in turn, been outdone by advanced synthesizers, which not only replicate piano sounds and maintain pressure sensitivity but can also mimic hundreds of other instruments—including the pipe organ. Like humans against Espers, the analog and digital have been warring with each other for generations. And, like the Espers, the analog—for now at least—seems to be creeping toward extinction.

A pipe organ is the first sound you hear after you flip on the SNES to play *Final Fantasy VI*. The game's opening music is a series of six—yes, VI—pitches stacking on top of each other in slow succession, each one a perfect fourth away from the one preceding it (figure 3.1). The perfect fourth is not particularly special in itself—it's just a musical interval, the distance from C to F on a piano. But when you stack fourths on top of one another with nothing to undergird them, they start to get unstable. If one were to keep stacking and stacking, you'd hit all twelve notes in the chromatic scale before you circled back around to the first note in the sequence. Think of a Jenga tower: It's sturdy for a few levels, but the taller the tower gets, the less stable it becomes, and the more you expect it to crash down.

FF6 is a tower that crashes down. First it crashes musically, within the first few measures of the introduction. Then it crashes metaphorically and literally, in that Kefka's hubris and the instability he visits upon the planet—represented by the tower-lair he constructs for himself in the World of Ruin—crashes down to the ground. The collapse of the organ music, after those first six notes, is rendered in two ponderous, dissonant chords. On screen, lightning flashes in a charcoal-grey sky, and "FINAL FANTASY III" appears in flaming letters.

The beginning of the game, the stacking pitches on the organ, gestures toward the end. The game's final battle, where this very music repeats itself, gestures toward the beginning. Humanity repeated its mistake with the War of the Magi, and the music repeats, too. Maybe in another thousand years, humanity will dust the organ off for a threepeat.

Figure 3.1 "Opening Theme" from Final Fantasy VI,
*mm. 1–10 (organ). Watch the Jenga tower build in the
first six measures, then collapse in the next four.*

Uematsu's instrumentation throughout the game
reflects a contrast of acoustic and digital, balance and
ruin. His use of pipe organs, electric instruments, and
synthesizers closely correlates with the unnatural use of
magic, evil, and the apocalypse. Electronic instruments
feature in every piece of battle music; from the oft-heard
"Battle Theme," in which a distorted electric guitar riffs
in the background; to "The Decisive Battle," in which a
Hammond organ leads with the melody; to "The Fierce
Battle," in which the primary melody is played on a
synthesizer; to "Dancing Mad," the final battle music,
which features both a pipe and Hammond organ.

Synthesized instruments also figure in heavily
when a confrontation with Kefka is imminent: in in
the Magitek Factory ("Devil's Lab"), before Kefka tries
to convince the heroes that Celes has been working
as a double agent; on the Floating Continent ("New

Continent"), before Kefka seizes control of the ancient statues and sets off the apocalypse; and in Kefka's Tower ("Last Dungeon"), the final area the player explores. With the exception of Uematsu's signature omnipresent electric bass, organs and electronic instruments appear rarely in other places, and are never associated with the heroes directly. (For the purposes of this discussion, let's count "Techno de Chocobo" as a running series gag and not as a reflection of Chocobos as ostriches of the damned.)

This kind of thoughtfulness is laced throughout *FF6*, in the painting of portraits, landscapes, events, and ideas—nouns, basically. It's not just the presence or absence of organs and synthesizers; it's the other astute choices in instrumentation, the way his melodies and harmonies reflect their subjects. Whether we as listeners actively pick up on these choices or not, they impact the way we interpret the story, take in the sights, and relate to the principal characters, each of whom has their own fully realized theme song—the most important device in the game's soundtrack, one that pole-vaults us across that Mario Pit.

Cyan

Doma, an insular kingdom in the East, is battle-scarred and under siege. When the player arrives on scene,

Imperial troops are beginning their final surge toward the castle gate—they're just a step away from taking the kingdom once and for all. A sentry reports to his superior inside the keep: The latest wave will be too much for them to hold back. Doma will fall. From offscreen, a shout: "A moment, Sir!"

A man strides onscreen: heavy-lidded eyes, black hair pulled back in a ponytail, bare arms, armor and boots in deep blue. It is Cyan, the knight/retainer to the king, an unparalleled swordsman. He steps between the two soldiers and, as though asking them to dance, says, "Allow me the honor!" Then he bursts through the gate and singlehandedly dispatches the entire Imperial contingent.

·

Cyan and his compatriots are coded as "other." The kingdom's sentries and troops wear powder blue turbans and boots and pale green robes that hit above the knee. Cyan's sprite has eyes a pixel narrower than the other characters, and he is the only character in the game with black hair. His speech is formal and archaic, leaning heavily on "thou," and he and his fellow Domans show unmatched deference to their king.

Cyan's theme is led by the shakuhachi, an end-blown bamboo flute closely associated with spiritual practice during Japan's feudal history. Beyond the shakuhachi, the piece is undergirded by a booming, low timpani, likely meant to represent taiko drums, and a regular jingle of handheld *suzu* bells, a sleigh bells–like instrument used during Shinto ceremony. This music—peppered with instruments not typically found in Western orchestras—marks Cyan and his kingdom as "others" as much as his appearance does. To clarify, this interpretation comes from an American gaze: A Japanese audience may read Cyan and hear his music in a very different way.

In the first half of the theme, the melody alternates between sustained notes and quick movements (figure 3.2), swishing and steadying with a fencer's precision—a kind of musical *iaido* demonstration. The harmony does not change, middle-register strings pulse steadily, and low strings and percussion sound in a distinct, repetitive rhythm—all implying constancy, even conservatism. This bears out in the script: His archaic speech, his discomfort with machinery and technology, and his buttoned-up sexuality heighten this conservatism to comic proportions. But he is also the sole keeper of his people's memory and traditions, and the steadiness of these opening measures, coupled with the unique instrumentation, speak to this sacred burden.

Figure 3.2 "Cyan" from Final Fantasy VI,
mm. 1–8 (shakuhachi).

Doma Castle's water source is an architectural feature. It's built over and into a river. After Cyan's victory over the Imperial contingent, the nearby Imperial camp goes abuzz with activity and Doma's waters turn an angry fuchsia. Almost immediately, the citizens begin to double over in agony, then collapse, some of them tumbling over the parapets to the stone pavement stories below. It's a chilling sight. By this point in the game, the gap between the player and the game world has closed far enough that these 16-bit sprites are real as humans. This is genocide, and the player is helpless to stop it.

Cyan runs to the king, whose vision has left him, and whose every breath is like fire in his lungs. He dies with Cyan at his side. Cyan and a single surviving sentry split up to look for survivors, but the sentry is never seen again. Doma is extinct.

•

The music's chilly formality only lasts through its first section. It doesn't melt away; it sublimates. There is a short bridge during which the pace doubles—in the pulsing strings, in the rhythm of the shakuhachi—with a feeling of impatience or building pressure. In the third and final section, the shakuhachi and the steadiness disappear entirely. The contrast is unexpected and magical.

What the player hears is a romantic reinvention of the first section's melody, played over fluttering woodwinds—this is the part that recalls Tchaikovsky's *Romeo and Juliet*. Cyan has suffered tremendous personal loss already, and it doesn't end with his people and his king. During his search for survivors, he finds his wife dead, and pulls his son's body hopelessly out of bed. The romanticism of the theme's final section reflects abiding love—for Doma and for his family—but it's tinged with unspeakable grief. As the romantic cycles endlessly toward the traditional and back, the music suggests a polite but futile instinct to avoid overt displays of emotion. When he discovers the remains of his family, he can only utter, "Dear me…"

Cyan is a deeply layered character, but his depth may not come through in the first half of the script: His archaisms, his discomfort around women, and his ineptitude with machinery are used most often as punchlines. Thinking about the pain he carries with him breaks my heart, yet it plays only a small part in the main plot. The optional storylines in the second half of the game are where we see his whole self: a man who crafts silk flowers and writes poetry for a bereaved woman, who reads up on machinery, who keeps a hidden stash of racy photos. You explore his subconscious and plumb into his grief by literally entering his dreams. All of this character development is optional—unless you find him on his secluded mountaintop and take him back to his ruined kingdom, you won't capture it all.

His theme music, then, is the principal way you learn who he is. His melody spans just over an octave and a half—a respectable range for an opera aria. This breadth reflects, in a delicate, subliminal way, his range of roles on screen: father, husband, widower, comic relief, savior, and protector. To my ear, it contains the starkest contrast of any of the characters' musical portraits. Every other theme, as it moves from section to section, maintains a clear personality: The gambler Setzer's stays heart-pounding, the secretive Strago's stays suspicious. Even Terra's theme, moving from cool to warm as Terra morphs between human and Esper, retains its march-like quality. Cyan's, though, drops its sword and kneels.

Relm

Relm is a remarkable ten-year-old: a supremely gifted painter and, though human, an heir of generations of magical abilities. Her grandfather, Strago, is a grizzled monster hunter and zoömancer—but Relm's work isn't with animals. Her magic is art. She renders her subjects so vividly that, when she sketches monsters on the battlefield, her work comes to life and fights back against its subject. This is a fitting power for a character who stirs up so much trouble: She sneaks out of the house, pulls pranks, throws precocious barbs at the other characters—and one time she paints a portrait of a sexy goddess, and her painting becomes possessed by a demon, and the painting nearly kills everyone. Usual kid stuff.

When she's introduced to the player, she runs down the stairs of her grandfather's house, interrupts his conversation with the other characters, and accidentally spills the beans about her family's magic abilities—kept secret from the rest of the world. The player hears immediately that there's more to her than impetuousness. Her music is darling and downcast, and her title card reads, "In her pictures she captures everything: forests, water, light… the very essence of life."

It's all so incongruous with the cheeky child the player meets. Based on the script and direction, we might expect a saucy, upbeat number. Instead, we get loveliness. We might expect her title card to describe an energetic, impulsive kid. Instead, it reads like a translation of Wang Wei's tranquil poem "Deer Park." Relm reads that way, too, once you get to know her; her impudence veils simple, abiding love for her grandfather. In the World of Ruin, she betrays her secret affection for Strago when she wiles him into fulfilling his lifelong goal of defeating Hidon, the unbeatable monster. In the final battle with Kefka, she proudly admits that she fights for her brave grandpa. And, in the post-credits sequence, she expresses a sincere wish to preserve him in portrait—one that probably won't murder him.

There are deeper elements shaping Relm's character. Her mother died when she was quite young, leaving behind a memento ring. This may be the only souvenir Relm still has of her mother. Her father abandoned her not much later. That pain is still fresh—she relives it in her onscreen nightmares: She curls up on the floor, crying for her father to come back; her dog barks at her, then dashes out the door to chase after him; Strago looks down at her silently. It's possible that—in her first moments onscreen, bounding down the stairs—she's hoping against hope that her dad will be there. (He is—but unrecognizably, in the guise of the ninja Shadow.)

It's easy to overlook Relm as you play through the game. At first blush, she seems to be a stock sassy tween, still watermarked by Shutterstock. Compare this to Cyan's time on screen, when the player gets to know him a bit, even without the optional World-of-Ruin follow-up. Learning the entirety of Relm's story is completely optional, and it's impossible to do so in one playthrough. Just as the Floating Continent falls, the player has to make a nail-biting decision that determines whether Shadow lives or plummets to his doom. If the player chooses to save him, they will never get to see Relm's recurring nightmare; if the player chooses to leave him, they never get to see her father's.

Because Relm joins the party last—and because her in-battle talent is fun in theory, but not all that useful in practice—it's easy to brush past her without much thought.

Her theme song, however, softly asks you to take a second look. Its first twelve measures are harmonically static—starting, and sticking to, F-sharp major. A flute, oboe, and bagpipe play a series of gentle, descending fragments spaced widely apart. The effect is sweet, but immature—not quite cohering the way an adult might hope it would. There's room for imagination—or frustration—between each fragment. You might find yourself asking: Where is this going?

The melody's somewhat baffling loveliness may distract you from its predominantly downward motion. Its eyes are cast on the floor, not out of shyness—Relm is absolutely not shy—but out of sadness. That descending fragment is repeated insistently and irregularly, alternating with a pattern that turns over on itself (figure 3.3). The pattern's repetition suggests she revisits, relives, and rethinks this sadness often. It has always interested me that the theme contains broad measure-and-a-half spans without any melodic motion—"Deer Park" stillness. Maybe this stillness is time stretching out in front of her, as it does when you're a child; maybe it's daylight; or maybe she's stepping back from her canvas, thumb to her chin.

Figure 3.3 "Relm" from Final Fantasy VI, *mm. 1–3 (flute/oboe). The two groups of notes here represent the descending and tumbling patterns; they repeat or echo themselves throughout the first section of the piece.*

In the final eight measures, a duet between oboe and bassoon finally introduces some cohesion but, as this happens, the piece changes key into a melancholy D-sharp minor. Still sweet, but darker and tenderer—a bruised pear in a still-life. Relm has suffered too much for a ten-year-old, and this is where we really start to feel it. The melody cuts unexpectedly deep, and the harmonies begin to flow in a way they didn't before. The surprise of this turn is what makes it heartbreaking—the tears came from nowhere. But they don't linger: The melody rises with hope, a measure of eighth notes tilts back and forth—a shrug of the shoulders, a playful twirl, or a steadying on a balance beam—and two half notes sigh, comforted, before the piece loops back to the beginning.

Relm's melody, fragmented as it is, spans just under an octave and a half—similar in range to Cyan's. This subtlety reflects a depth of character too easily overlooked. Her music aptly mixes grace with doubt, pain with promise. Light and dark, grey and color.

Uematsu has said that Relm is his favorite character, and it makes sense for him to have an affinity for the young artist. He has Relm's magic in him somewhere, in his gift of giving life through his work. He picks the right colors, makes the lines sharp and clean, and gets the framing just so. Through this instinct, he renders characters with remarkable, moving efficiency. Relm's theme is just twenty measures long, but it tells us a complicated story. It's childlike without being childish. It's a deft illustration: a precocious painter, a soft heart, a skinned knee.

Shadow

Of the game's protagonists, Shadow is the most laconic (excepting Gogo, the agender mimic who speaks three lines to introduce themself, then never again). He floats in and out of the party at his own discretion, sometimes only participating if he's paid. By way of introduction, we're told "He'd slit his mama's throat for a nickel." A player can start and finish the game without learning a thing about Shadow's complicated history; nothing about it is explicit in the first half of the game. If you play your cards wrong, he'll disappear on the Floating Continent—and you'll never learn who he is. Shadow is more than a nameless mercenary. He's a man on the run from himself.

His given name is Clyde. As a young man, he formed a train-robbing duo with his friend Baram. As they celebrated a particularly successful heist, they jointly adopted "Shadow" as their nom de crime. The next job went horrifyingly wrong: The two were on the run, in danger of being caught, and Baram was mortally wounded. He begged Clyde to take a knife and put him out of his misery, but Clyde was shaken by the idea and couldn't bring himself to kill his friend. He sprinted away instead, leaving Baram to die alone, in pain, crying for mercy. The guilt still racks Shadow when the player meets him more than a decade later.

Shadow's past bubbles up through a series of achronological, randomly occurring dreams, only viewable in the anything-goes second half of the game. These complement Relm's, and only after seeing into both characters' pasts can the player finally trace the line from father to daughter.

In one dream, Clyde stumbles, half-dead, into a familiar village square, where a dog finds him and fetches a young woman for help. In another, he is walking away from a familiar home—the very home Relm shares with her grandfather, Strago. His dog follows him out of town. "You came to fetch me," Shadow says. "But I won't be going back. I want you, and the girl, to live in a peaceful world." He keeps the dog, but orphans his daughter quick as a knife slices.

In a final nightmare—I can't help but think must be recurring—Baram implores Clyde to join him in death.

•

To paint Shadow through music, Uematsu pays homage to Ennio Morricone's work, specifically from the Dollars trilogy—*A Fistful of Dollars* (1964), *For a Few Dollars*

More (1965), and *The Good, the Bad, and the Ugly* (1966). He mashes up elements from each of these three movies' theme songs (the omnipresent whistle, the strum of a guitar, the mouth harp) to create an instantly recognizable reference that captures Shadow's withdrawn, prickly personality, recalling Clint Eastwood's iconic stone-faced screen presence. He doesn't wear a poncho and smoke cigarillos like Eastwood, but, like a stock character from old Westerns, he does have a background in train robbery. Then there's the connection with Eastwood's role, the Man with No Name: Shadow didn't just adopt his name to hide his identity; in the original Japanese script of *FF6*, Shadow tells the other heroes, "I'm a man who threw away his name." (Ted Woolsey translated this line for the SNES as "I've forsaken the world.") Shadow wants to become no one.

A Fistful of Dollars was an unlicensed remake of Akira Kurosawa's *Yojimbo* (1961), about a dark-robed ronin. This cowboy music, repurposed for a mysterious ninja, traces a line back to Kurosawa, who himself borrowed heavily from American Westerns. Uematsu acknowledges and exploits this loop of references to create a razor-sharp portrait: Within a few measures, we learn that Shadow will be enigmatic, distant, and mercenary—and that he's capable of impressive acts of heroism.

Shadow's special ability in battle is "Throw." He can toss shuriken, knives, and short swords at enemies to cause massive amounts of damage. This talent makes sense for a ninja, but also for Shadow's character: He can throw items away in battle, including the game's most powerful and priceless weapons. He threw his partner, his daughter, and his name away. One way or another, he throws himself away. His "Throw" allows him to keep as cool a distance from his targets as he keeps from the other heroes, and it acquits him of delivering a fatal wound face to face.

Unexpectedly, Shadow performs several acts of generosity and self-sacrifice. When prodded, he offers taut advice on love and grief to other characters. He helps the martial artist Sabin, a total stranger, infiltrate the Imperial base at Doma. He (usually) sticks with Sabin and Cyan to board, and escape from, the Phantom Train—a terrifying, sentient manifestation of death (and an unsubtle callback to Shadow's past). On the Floating Continent, he saves a life—that of Celes, the former Imperial general and onetime soprano. Then he stays behind to stymie Kefka so the other heroes can get away safely.

•

Shadow and Relm are pretty different: Relm is "forests, water, light," and her father is a shade who "comes and goes like the wind." Light opposite dark. Wind through the trees and over the water. They are different but entangled. The up-and-down eighth notes in the father's music have the same nose as those in the daughter's (figure 3.4), but the overall resemblance is thin—different rhythms, different placement, different dispositions. The F-sharp major key of Relm's theme is just a step away from Shadow's E minor—very close—but the keys have no real relationship with each other outside their proximity. Shadow and Relm come so close to each other in-game—they can explore together and fight together, if the player wants them to, and when they are idle they hang out with the rest of the crew belowdecks in an airship. But they never speak or interact. Related, but never relating.

Figure 3.4 "Shadow" from Final Fantasy VI, *mm. 5–8 (whistle). The two bracketed passages reflect their lettered counterparts in Relm's theme. They have extremely similar melodic outlines, though their rhythms and meter are reworked.*

During the escape from the Floating Continent, you have a choice: You can make the heroes jump to their airship as quickly as possible, leaving Shadow behind to die, or you can risk it and wait for him before you take the leap—he catches up mere seconds before the fall. The choice is brutal: On the first playthrough, you don't know what will happen if that countdown clock reaches zero. Will Shadow show up? Will the heroes die waiting for him? If they die, will you have to hack your way through the punishing Floating Continent stage again? If Shadow is left behind, will he find his own way to survive? The cruelty of this choice mirrors the awful choice that Clyde had to make about Baram: Will you risk yourself, shaking with anxiety, for mercy on your friend—or will you cut and run?

The choice is real: Shadow will disappear from the game if the player doesn't wait. I didn't wait when I first played through, and I felt his disappearance in my gut for the rest of the game. I hoped to find him somewhere in the ruined world, but all I found was a ghost in my roster and a conspicuous absence during the game's curtain call. It haunted me, in its own little way.

If he lives through to the final battle, Shadow confesses to Kefka that he finally understands friendship and family. That's why he chooses to fight. But after Kefka is defeated, as his tower is collapsing, there's no more fighting to be done. His last big job, as professed in his dream—to leave his daughter Relm in a peaceful world—is complete.

And so Shadow goes on the lam for the last time, lagging slightly behind his comrades, then nestling himself unnoticed in a corner. He knows his death will go unacknowledged and unseen, just as his suffering friend's did. "Baram! I'm going to stop running. I'm going to begin all over again…"

·

Shadow's theme, like all the other heroes', is recalled in the endgame medley. It plays during his final moments—not just his final moments on screen, but his final moments of life. Instead of a whistle, the melody is played by the strings; instead of a strummed guitar, cascading arpeggios on the harp; instead of the twang of a mouth harp, the cry of French horns. The lonely stoicism of the Morriconesque theme is split at the sternum, exposing a raw, beating heart. Unlike the silent cowboys who precede him, who may stride coolly offscreen, Shadow faces his demons. Perhaps it's because of this reckoning that he chooses to die—a rare, tragic denouement of clenched-jaw masculinity.

Uematsu has crafted a tremendously elastic melody, stretching effortlessly from tumbleweeds to chrysanthemums. That Western-movie sound is a pinpoint-specific pop-culture reference, a treatment none of the other characters' themes receive. Yet it transforms in the ending medley, shedding its roots to blend in seamlessly with the other characters' themes. The music's stoicism melts away to convey grief, guilt, compassion, and resolve in one quick jab. Shadow, himself a pop-culture trope, becomes more like his comrades and less like Clint Eastwood as he gains a name, a past, and a heart. What remarkable sleight-of-hand to turn such worn material—a strong-but-silent warrior, the music of dust-beaten men drawing their pistols—into something so gut-wrenching and complicated. If you take the time to look closely—and both he and the game work hard at making inspection difficult—you see that Shadow wears twenty different shades of black.

Landscapes

Uematsu's musical landscapes are as evocative as his portraits: full of whip-smart choices and references that reinforce what's onscreen and telegraph what isn't. There's the coal-mining town Narshe's jazzy looseness, now and then sounding a quick-exhaled breath as a kind of soft percussion—the soft puffs of steam we make when we breathe out in the cold. Machinery onscreen here and there emits its own steam, and Narshe's coal powers the game-world's steam engines. The loose harmonies hint at Narshe's uneasy neutrality in the war, the underground operation of the resistance, the constant threat of invasion.

The Magitek Factory's theme, "Devil's Lab," also gives an immediate sense of place. Uematsu's use of synthesizers to indicate artificiality and evil, and to hint that a confrontation with Kefka is on the horizon, is front-and-center. The piece begins with a steady beat of industrial sound effects—mechanical clicks and anvil-like clangs—then a killer bass-synth riff (figure 3.5). It may be the stankiest groove in video game music history, rolling and locking like someone doing the robot. Robot is pretty much the idea—together, the bass and percussion create a conveyor belt–like motion that rolls the rest of the music steadily forward. Whooshes and buzzing alto synths, like beeps of a computer and swings of a mechanical arm, accent the music's brass melody. A string section wanders in, looking up and down, mesmerized, watching it all as if through a window. Onscreen are actual conveyor belts, crane-arms, and ducts. Everything is riveted steel. It's a grinning Trent Reznor cameo, or a funk that transforms the whole scene into the music video of Janet Jackson's "Rhythm Nation."

Figure 3.5 "Devil's Lab" from Final Fantasy VI,
*mm. 5–8 (synth bass). Absolute banger. The bracketed
section, with its five-note, upward, minor scale lightly
recalls Kefka's theme.*

It's so much fun, in fact, that one might forget how
sinister a place this is. The ducts and conveyor belts and
steel are built on the backs of living beings. Espers are
kept in glass tubes like captured beetles—their life is
drained and their exhausted bodies are dumped into
garbage pits. The laboratory part of "Devil's Lab" is clear
from the first measure of music; the devil reveals itself
only slowly.

Then there's the distinguishing sounds of the World
of Balance and the World of Ruin. The overworld
themes' contrast is the starkest: Terra's grassy theme
music, which plays during exploration of the World of
Balance, is replaced by "Dark World"—a dour, plodding
number for pipe organ, clavichord, tubular bell, and
whistling wind. Where the land had been spring green
and deep blue, it's now dun plains with bruise-purple
waters. The World of Balance's pan flute is sounded by
human breath; the World of Ruin's organ bleakly sucks
in the air from its surroundings.

In the World of Balance, free towns are scored by "Kids Run Through the City," a pastoral piece in a triple meter, cradled by a flute, acoustic guitar, and strings. Ruin towns have the utterly cheerless "The Day After." This one is still fronted by a flute, but this time with a wailing oboe and weeping mandolin. It sounds like a reject from the *Godfather* soundtrack, and calls to mind New York's early 20th-century Italian ghettos. The town's maps haven't changed, but their music has. And their colors—like their spirits—have dimmed considerably.

In one last grand contrast, the World of Balance's airship music sounds like a Showcase Showdown on *The Price is Right*—you've just won a five-day, four-night stay at a resort in sunny Bali!—where Ruin's is the cold, wispy opening of a dour soap opera.

Rather than simply recycling music from the first half of the game to the second, as some composers might, Uematsu reinvented. This is part of the ingenuity of the game's soundtrack. It resists sameness in ways many of its contemporaries and predecessors didn't; and that specificity breathes a unique life into each environment. "Devil's Lab" is only heard one time in the game, and then it disappears forever: You can't go back to the Magitek Factory after your first visit because you blow it up on your way out. Because of the music's singularity, though—and its funky bassline—the factory looms large in the player's memory long after it's gone.

The Phantom Train

The Phantom Train delivers souls from the material world to the afterlife. Early in the game, you accidentally board it while it's parked at its platform in the Phantom Forest, then you must find a way to get off the train before it reaches the afterlife. Only when the train delivers you back to your origin in the woods do you see how grim it truly is: You are forced to watch the murdered people of Doma slowly file aboard.

Your time on the train is set to the tune of an almost-but-not-quite jazzy minor-key waltz, jump started by some ambient train sound effects. Ballroom music feels appropriate for the train's Belle Époque–styled cars, but the harmonies are a little twisted, and though it's technically a quick *vivace*—about 163 beats per minute—it feels like a ponderous *largo*. In the complete absence of living beings, there are no dancers to track across the floor and no way to know if this waltz should feel quick or lumbering. The lives of the souls on this train—were they too fast or too slow? That the music is forced to loop over and over again does nothing to lessen its inexorability. As the train's ghosts so aptly put it: "N.o…e.s.c.a.p.e…!"

Dance music, in this context, nods toward the *danse macabre*, the idea that we are all dancing toward certain doom. Camille Saint-Saëns's famous *Danse macabre* (1874) is probably the most well-known musical rendering of this idea, and it also has a distinctly waltzy meter and melody. But "Phantom Train" is closer in spirit to one of Shostakovich's "jazz" waltzes—which, though they do sound a bit spooky to the modern ear, are not explicitly death-related.

The Phantom Train is an insistent *memento mori*—a tangible reminder that we're all gonna die: A train, after all, travels in only one direction, and on a predetermined, unchangeable course. That the characters accidentally trap themselves onboard is another bony elbow to the chest. Bodiless, white-robed ghosts wisp to and fro over the red and gold carpet, and their presence does nothing to lessen your disquietude. Some volunteer to fight alongside you temporarily, some try to kill you, and some peddle basic provisions—commerce is certain even in the great beyond.

To escape the train, Sabin, Shadow, and Cyan must destroy the engine car in a battle—but in order to fight it, they have to get in front of it: The boss fight takes place with the trio running ahead of the engine car, on the tracks, turning around to strike it when they can. Three people trying to outrun and destroy an unstoppable steam-engine Grim Reaper: Has any video game ever *mementoed* so much *mori*?

Sabin, with his extensive training in the martial arts, is famously capable of performing a suplex on the train's engine car, whisking it up in the air and crashing it back down onto the ground. I doubt that, when the developers programmed Sabin's special abilities, they envisioned him body-slamming a hundred-ton person-ification of death, but it's certainly the most fun thing to do with that skill. For that brief moment in the sky, death is suspended, and you and Sabin are invincible, everlasting.

•

The train's music mirrors the journey through the train itself. It begins with a gentle guitar prelude (becoming an interlude after the first loop), then surprises with a shockingly loud brass melody: sudden death! The first phrase of the melody is an unbroken line in the brass. The second phrase is split in two, ending in a pattern of twelve notes—the stroke of midnight, perhaps—broken away from the rest of the phrase by a quarter rest. The pattern holds steady on a B-flat for nine of the twelve strokes, then drives suggestively downward into an E (figure 3.6). The B-flat pitch itself is significant—it's a tritone away from the tonic E, the piece's central pitch. In

European classical music, the tritone interval is known as *diabolus in musica*, or "the devil in music," because of its dissonant quality. It isn't very easy on the ears. The tritone is associated with death and evil—Saint-Saëns's *Danse macabre* also plays with the interval. Uematsu is really hammering this theme home.

After two statements of the primary melody, the strings wail through a hysterical descending passage. They're interrupted by a two-note blare from the brass—then they repeat their complaint note for note. Are the strings falling into the grave? Or are they trying to claw their way out of it, stomped back down by the trumpets? Who's piling the dirt on top?

Figure 3.6 "Phantom Train" from Final Fantasy VI, *mm. 25–31 (trumpet).*

Despite their resistance, the strings must yield to the quiet strum of the guitar, and the cycle must begin again, then again, then again. It's cartoonish, over-the-top morbidity. Think of "The Skeleton Dance," Disney's 1929 cartoon short, in which skeletons skip about and do the Charleston in lo-fi black-and-white. For economy, lots of the animation in the short is seen again, then again, then again—just as, for function, the music in this game must loop. But the looping feels almost intentional here: For the roughly thirty minutes of time the player spends on the Phantom Train, the music drills again, then again, then again. It is always present, always plodding forward. It might be diverted temporarily by battle sequences, but until we figure out how to body-slam Death, it will return to claim us—again, then again, then again.

Though *Final Fantasy VI* can be wacky, it doesn't make a joke out of grief. Even the near-comic absurdity of the Phantom Train disappears in the face of genuine loss. The game's cast is large and diverse, but they are united by trauma—if not the loss of loved ones, then the loss of the world as they know it. They all cope in different ways: through nightmares, visions, obsession, withdrawal, found family, and arts and crafts. They also rise against their grief—or because of it—to fight for what they believe in.

This sequence on the ghost train is more than a whimsical spook. Consider Shadow: He is a former train robber whose partner's death is an open wound. What does this journey mean for him? He doesn't utter a word about it—but his presence doesn't feel like an accident.

More important is what this moment means for Cyan, who sees his wife and child boarding the train and is offered one last, torturous chance to say goodbye. After the train departs, Cyan stands at the end of the platform, just in front of the clocktower, staring quietly downward.

As Sabin, the player paces up and down the platform, anxious to move on to the next part of the game. But no matter how hard Sabin prods, Cyan won't utter a word. Shadow asks you to shut up and keep still. As is the game's apocalypse, this is one of few completely soundless moments, and for good reason. The silence weighs heavier here than any music could.

LEITMOTIF

A MOTIF IS ANY RECOGNIZABLE snippet of music that repeats over time—think of the famous first four notes of Beethoven's Fifth. Leitmotif is a narrower term: It's typically used in the context of of a dramatic work like a movie, opera, or musical. It takes the motif concept one step further. It not only associates a fragment of music with a specific character, place, or idea, but often evolves or changes in some way as a story progresses, thus advancing the drama. The advancement of a leitmotif (and consequent dramatic advancement) can happen in a number of ways: The leitmotif can appear in new dramatic situations, dragging its subject along with it; it can combine with another leitmotif, linking two subjects together; or it can itself evolve, changing in melody or rhythm to reflect change. Leitmotifs can indicate or reflect a twist in the story, help develop a character, call up characters or ideas that don't appear onstage or onscreen, hint at unseen motives or emotions, or associate other-wise unrelated subjects.

As we listen to and digest leitmotif, we're listening to and digesting change—that's what makes it worth studying.

If we think of character or place themes as unidimensional pinpoints showing us where we are or whom we're looking at, we can think of leitmotifs as two-dimensional lines, pulling our pinpoints into slopes and intersections. From the careful arithmetic and algebra that goes into constructing a motif, leitmotif introduces trigonometry and calculus. Plenty of ballets, operas, musicals, and movies assign melodic fragments to onscreen or onstage counterparts, so its use is familiar to us even if we never noticed or knew the name for it. As the 90s progressed, the leitmotif became a more common technique in video game music.

The technique is strongly associated with Richard Wagner, the 19th-century composer famous for his hefty dramatic operas—especially his *Der Ring des Nibelungen*, a cycle of four massive operas whose cumulative performance length is about fifteen hours. (If you figure in intermissions, the whole affair can run a little longer than the theatrical releases of the Lord of the Rings and Hobbit trilogies combined.) There are hundreds of leitmotifs in this cycle; musicologists are still picking it apart. But Wagner doesn't own leitmotif—he didn't even like the term—and plenty of other composers have famously used it. In John Williams's scores from the Star Wars films, for example, there are leitmotifs for Luke, Darth Vader, the Empire, the Force, and even for Han and Leia's relationship. They recur in various permutations, over different harmonies, in different orchestrations, and in different situations as the story goes. When a composer employs leitmotif as a compositional device, the drama happens not just through the script or book or libretto, not just on the stage or screen, but in the music. Whether or not we're cognizant of it, the recurrence of leitmotifs helps us learn, remember, and revise our understanding of the subjects they represent.

Final Fantasy VI's character leitmotifs are the most common and the easiest to pick up on in the game. Typically, even when they've been transformed, they retain the most of their shape and are readily identifiable. For example, each theme is iterated in at least two separate places in the game: first on its own, usually when the character is introduced and their title card appears on screen; and second, in a medley as part of the endgame cutscene—maybe with different instruments or at a different speed. Many characters have their themes crop up in other places, too. A few characters have their primary themes restated beginning to end, lightly reworked, for an effect that contrasts their main counterpart. Other heroes' themes are chopped up and sprinkled here and there as the situation calls for it.

Truly understanding Uematsu's use of leitmotif, why it's effective, and why it's celebrated, requires more than picking apart a single scrap of music. It requires identifying a motif's recurrence, contrasting the way two or more occurrences sound and how they're used, then figuring out what that means for the story. Understanding the meaning of a motif versus a leitmotif is like understanding the difference between speed and acceleration. It's not just measuring movement, it's measuring the movement of movement.

Locke

Locke is pathologically heroic—and so is his theme music. If we're sticking with John Williams over Richard Wagner: Locke's theme has the same bold, exciting air as the themes from the Indiana Jones or Superman movies. By trade, Locke is a thief (although he prefers the euphemism "treasure hunter"). His theme leaps straight out of the speaker—with no warm up or introduction—in the exact way Locke jumps into adventure after adventure. Right out of the gate, you hear his excessive excitement—the percussion becomes a little unhinged in the third measure (figure 4.1), tumbles over itself, and the melody swings out of its native key, like a vine over a ravine, in the fifth measure (figure 4.2). You don't get the impression that Locke or his theme have run fully off the rails or lost touch with reality; they're just a smidge manic. Locke's fits of brashness and thievery come from a fearless, well-intentioned heart—reflected, perhaps, in the heartbeat-like rhythmic pattern in the strings and percussion. His heart is the crux of his character arc: It's permanently broken. His state of perpetual derring-do helps him evade confronting his grief and self-blame.

Figure 4.1 "Locke" from Final Fantasy VI, *mm. 1–4 (snare). The bracketed notes represent those accented off the beat, creating that slightly unhinged sound.*

Figure 4.2 "Locke" from Final Fantasy VI, *mm. 1–8 (strings, melody only). The circled note, an F-natural, is the only note in the opening measures outside the key of G major—again slightly unhinged—and hints at the key change that leads into the piece's final section.*

Locke was indirectly involved in an accident that caused his fiancée, Rachel, to fall from a bridge, suffer a head injury, and come down with a soap-operatic case of amnesia. She forgot who he was, and his attempts to help jog her memory caused her so much distress that her father permanently banished Locke from her presence. During his exile, the Empire invaded Rachel's hometown and she was killed, but—gasp!—she recovered her memory and declared her love for Locke with her dying breaths. Locke blames himself for not being there to protect her, and that turns his natural proclivity for adventure-seeking into an obsession. He copes by compulsively protecting every woman he meets—including Terra and Celes, the two adult women protagonists, both of whom are powerful enough not to need his protection.

He also copes by paying a strange man to keep Rachel in suspended animation in his basement, which is extremely normal.

"Forever Rachel" plays during the flashback showing Rachel's accident. It's mostly a reiteration of Locke's theme music, shifted into a minor key and slowed down, but it's been broken and reassembled like a dropped vase—most of the pieces are there, but they never quite line up the same as before (figures 4.3–4.5). With a few tiny changes, the overenthusiastic theme becomes doleful and listless. This is leitmotif at its most fundamental: Locke's theme is modified to associate him with Rachel's death, adding dimension both to his character and to the melodrama unfolding onscreen.

Figure 4.3 "Locke" from Final Fantasy VI, *mm. 9–18 (strings and oboe, melody only). This, from the second half of Locke's theme, forms the beginning of "Forever Rachel" (figure 4.4).*

Figure 4.4 "Forever Rachel" from Final Fantasy VI,
mm. 1–10 (bassoon/flute/oboe melody, transposed).
*This, from the second half of Locke's theme, has been
transposed into a minor key, but otherwise virtually the
same—right down to the number of times fragment "a"
is repeated.*

Figure 4.5 "Forever Rachel" from Final Fantasy VI, *mm. 11–16 (flute). The primary melody of "Forever Rachel" draws note-for-note from the opening measures of Locke's theme—compare the bracketed section to figure 4.2. The theme diverges after the bracketed fragment, headed into its minor key, but continues to subtly mimic Locke's theme.*

In the World of Ruin, Celes—whom Locke grows to love throughout the game—wakes up on an island alone with Cid, an old friend and father figure. Cid falls ill and, depending on the player's actions, either lives or dies. If he dies, Celes is so grief-wracked, hopeless, and alone that she jumps from the island's cliffs. But instead of dying by suicide, she washes ashore. During a few moments without music, during which neither the player nor Celes knows quite what to feel, an injured bird lands on the shore, swathed in Locke's bandana.

"Forever Rachel" kicks in when Celes spots the bandana. Here is another example of leitmotif: This track, though it's unchanged from when we first hear it during Locke's flashback, is recontextualized to infuse the scene with meaning—and to take on some new meaning of its own. In this new context, the theme signals Celes's hope that the thief might be alive somewhere, bringing Locke into the scene even though he is not physically present. It reflects her thinking and influences the player's. The music itself begins to entangle hopelessness and hope. When Celes washes ashore, she still wishes she were dead—but she finds a glimmer of will in that bandana, and the player hears it. It's a longshot, but maybe her—our—old friends are out there somewhere, alive and breathing, waiting to be found.

The last time the player might hear "Forever Rachel" is when Locke restores a powerful artifact—the remains of the Esper Phoenix—to unlock its magic and finally wake Rachel from suspended animation. She lives just long enough to say goodbye to her beloved, and to absolve him of the guilt he harbors. She then gives up her body to fully restore the cracked Phoenix magicite, which teaches the player a spell to undo death.

In a brief scene with no music, Locke and Celes speak. "I feel lighter than air," he says at the end of their exchange. "Let's go! We have work to do!!"

Cue Locke's dashing main theme. If "Forever Rachel" were a shattered vase, here is where it's fully restored, just as the Phoenix magicite has been. The leitmotif is no longer simply describing Locke; it's telling us the story with Rachel has ended. The old Locke has been revived, strong as ever and ready for his next adventure. His theme is now about resilience as much as recklessness.

Without "Forever Rachel," Locke is just an off-the-shelf hero with baggage. Through the piece's contrast to the thief's main theme, we find a way to empathize with him. Perhaps we wouldn't go so far as to cryogenically freeze loved ones, but we all understand the impulse to preserve them—and, more selfishly, their presence in our lives—no matter the damage we might do to ourselves. Rachel's accident was Locke's emotional undoing. But, as we learn through leitmotif, Locke finally heals enough to find himself again.

In the end-of-game medley, Locke's theme inter-weaves with Celes's. This occurrence of the leitmotif musically consummates their relationship and hints to the player that they'll stick together after the game is over. Locke is no longer just a vessel for grief and guilt; he's no longer an injured bird with a blue bandana. He's done more than heal. He's relearned how to love.

Setzer

Setzer's theme is even more Williamsesque than Locke's, foregoing the neurosis for pure daredevilry. Setzer is a gambler and a pilot, and his theme music is sonic adren-aline: a trumpet melody that soars with quick-moving strings at the helm, barrel-rolling around the crash of cymbals and timpani. Like Locke's, Setzer's theme also receives a sepia-toned reimagining—this time as an epitaph for Daryl, a fellow thrill-seeking pilot and the gambler's late girlfriend. In their tragic backstory, the two were racing in their airships, flirting intermittently, when Daryl took the lead and then shot ahead toward the stars. She never returned home. Setzer discovered the wreckage of her ship, the Falcon, a year later.

You enter Daryl's tomb in the World of Ruin and descend into the underground hangar where the restored Falcon rests. Setzer relives his memories of Daryl. "Epitaph" plays. This melancholy remix of Setzer's theme is heard only in this scene—telling us this is an important and rare moment. "Epitaph" is paced slower than its counterpart, and its texture is far more modest. There's no percussion, a mellow acoustic guitar replaces the heart-pounding strings and trumpet, and a trio of flutes and a mandolin fill in the blanks. The sound echoes Led Zeppelin's "Stairway to Heaven," with its guitar and quartet of recorders. Apt, given the circumstances: The characters descend a stairway as Setzer's memories are played back—memories of a woman who physically flew toward the heavens before she died. The melody of "Epitaph"—the leitmotif—sticks pretty close to Setzer's theme, with a few changes in rhythm. Unlike "Forever Rachel," it keeps the original motif in a major key and a smattering of the same harmonies appear. It's the change in tempo and texture that shifts the music's meaning: The brash becomes tender; the cavalier becomes solemn.

This is Setzer's only soft moment in the game, and he desperately needs it. He is, objectively, a scumbag. He cashed in on the Empire's rise to power, he is introduced to the player during his plot to kidnap and possibly sexually assault an opera singer (a plan the party foils), and he joins the resistance only reluctantly. Setzer mentions Daryl just once before he decides to drag his friends through the monster-infested labyrinth that leads to her tomb, and—as with so many other important character development moments—it's in an easy-to-miss, casual, wholly optional conversation. Her story is extraneous. That is, it's extraneous until it suddenly becomes a compulsory plot point. The player must access the Falcon, must trudge through Setzer's memory, to beat the game. But it would have been just as easy a storytelling device for Setzer to have built a new airship post-apocalypse, which would nullify the need for Daryl completely. She exists only to humanize Setzer, as does the singular occurrence of "Epitaph." Without the development of his leitmotif in "Epitaph," he's just a scumbag. With it, he's a scumbag with a heart.

To his credit, Setzer reforms a bit once he meets the heroes. By the end of the game, he has to some extent atoned for his scumbaggery by putting it all on the line for the resistance: his body; his own aircraft, the Blackjack; and the Falcon, a keepsake of his late beloved. "Epitaph" nudges the Softer Side of Setzer™ ahead, paving the way for his leitmotif's gentle treatment in the endgame medley, which hammers his reformation home.

Interestingly, Setzer's music plays an outsize role at the end of the game, after the characters' medley has completed. The party races out of Kefka's collapsing tower on the Falcon, accompanied by a tensed-up version of his theme—this time not meant to indicate Setzer or Daryl directly, but to conjure up the adrenaline rush of a dangerous flight. As the credits roll, the Falcon dashes through the skies, flying over city after city as citizens look up in hope for the first time since their world ended. Setzer's theme blares in accompaniment—the leitmotif now drawing on the gambler's carefree attitude to become a victory anthem.

Gau

Gau is a bit of a mystery. The official guidebook *Final Fantasy Ultimania Archive* describes him as a "[p]ure and rambunctious wild child raised by monsters." Occupation: Feral Youth. He likes shiny things and dislikes clothes. He's an Aries and his blood type is B (unspecified if it is B+ or B-, but let's be grateful for what information we have). We wouldn't know some of this information without reading the *Ultimania*. (The game certainly never discloses his astrological sign or blood type.) We don't immediately understand who he is or where he comes from. All we have is the boy's title card: "Draped in monster hides, eyes shining with intelligence. A youth surviving against all odds…"

And, of course, we have his theme music.

At thirteen years old, Gau is the second-youngest person in our cast of characters. His mother died in childbirth, and his father, who suffers from an unspecified mental illness, tossed Gau out onto the Veldt—a vast, dangerous savanna—when the child was still an infant. He was raised by animals—by monsters. He's dressed in ragged hides. His language skills are limited. He is tempted into joining the heroes the way a dog might be tempted to follow someone home: They toss a piece of dried meat at him, and he follows them around forever after. He's a memorable source of comic relief: He jumps around the screen, makes funny sounds, hoards shiny things, plays practical jokes, and irritates the hell out of Cyan and Sabin.

Cyan and Sabin, lost on the Veldt, take Gau in because they believe he can locate a treasure that will help them reunite with their friends, who are currently on the other side of the planet. Gau does his schtick, then helps the heroes find the treasure. That could have been it for the little guy. But in the World of Ruin, the heroes finally make the connection between Gau and a strange old man who lives in a secluded cabin—his father.

The heroes decide to pull a *Queer Eye*: They make Gau over, provide lessons on etiquette, and stage a father-son reunion. But this doesn't have that TV-perfect ending. Dad doesn't recognize the dressed-up teenager he sees. Instead, the encounter triggers a memory of a dream the old man had—of tossing a demon child out onto the plain. Gau bows his head in disappointment, but outside the man's cabin a few moments later, his feelings sway toward the positive: "Fffatherrr…alive… H…a…p…p…y…"

As with the others, the depth of Gau's character depends on your thoroughness as a player. For even the most thorough of us, it's easy for the kid's wackiness to eclipse his sob story—so his theme music, seemingly incongruous, is a necessary storytelling device. It opts out of his wacky wildness and cuts straight to his back-story. The theme is an elegant sixteen-measure melody played on a cello, then repeated on a flute, backed up with strings and the flutter of a mandolin. The theme is unembellished, a little sad, and unfailingly sweet—and, once you get past his kookiness, so is Gau. You hear his primary theme music just twice: once when you first meet him, and again when he meets and is rejected by his father. Once to set it up, once to spike it over the net.

Gau's music is also embedded elsewhere in a curious way. When the player wanders across the Veldt, the usual overworld music is replaced by "Wild West." Because this savanna is Gau's home, "Wild West" functions as a kind of secondary theme for him—one that fully addresses the tamelessness that his main theme omits. It doesn't function, dramatically, the same way as "Forever Rachel" or "Epitaph," and the relationship between the two pieces isn't quite as obvious.

One of Uematsu's trademarks is drawing on global inspirations to efficiently communicate ideas of char-acter and place. The main feature of "Wild West" is a perfect example. The Veldt, a wild and dangerous place, is coded as a kind of pan-African landscape: hay-colored grass, a single acacia tree, dun-colored mountains across the horizon—it's a miscellaneous *National Geographic* cover photo. Uematsu's musical rendering of the landscape echoes this: The main feature of "Wild West" is its percussion, based vaguely on West African instruments and rhythms. But the similarities to traditional West African music end with the drums; the rest of the piece is played on an oboe and the score's ever-present strings. It's split into four sections. The first is a percussion solo, which is more elaborate on the second and subsequent loops. The second is a series of disconnected phrases in the strings. And in the third and fourth sections, the oboe joins the strings for two new melodic fragments. The tuned instruments leap and tumble as Gau does among the monsters.

Despite their stark differences, the music of the Veldt is quietly connected to Gau's "formal" theme music. The opening line of "Wild West" unexpectedly mimics the opening of Gau's theme. The contour loosely aligns in the first and second measures, the rhythm is exactly the same in the second measure, and the third measures both begin with steep downward motion (figures 4.6 and 4.7). "Wild West" clips, quickens, warps, or simplifies fragments of Gau's theme, but a bare resemblance remains. As the Veldt's music goes on, it resembles Gau's theme less and less, getting wilder with each passing section. It mirrors Gau's exile from humanity—hacking away at his leitmotif and using negative space as a window for us to glimpse his lost childhood.

Figure 4.6 "Gau" from Final Fantasy VI, *mm. 1–6 (flute).*

Figure 4.7 "Wild West" from Final Fantasy VI, *mm. 5–11. The "a" and "b" sections loosely align with those from Gau's theme.*

Where Setzer and Locke's leitmotifs soften but stay recognizable in "Epitaph" and "Forever Rachel," Gau's leitmotif brittles and breaks in "Wild West," distorting it almost beyond discernibility. The relationship between the two pieces may be barely noticeable on a casual listen, but the effect is real. You read Gau's title card and hear his melancholy main theme before you see him in action, so you necessarily perceive his wildness as a hide draped over his gentleness and innocence. Where secondary themes retcon some tragedy into Locke and Setzer's lives, the Veldt's music is a fundamental component of Gau's character. It sharpens its fangs, takes up the boy's humanity, and gnaws it to the bone.

Terra

Terra is the first character the player meets. For this reason alone, it feels like she could be the game's principal hero—and indeed the first half of the game (and much of its music) revolves around her. She is the key to the fight against the Empire, not only because she possesses the gift of magic, but because she can do something no other characters can: convince the Espers to join the fight. Aspects of her life are mirrored in those of other characters. Like Setzer and Celes, she represents good as a conscious choice. As half-Esper, she possesses tremendous magical power; as half-human she is capable of grossly misusing that power—but she chooses not to. Like Gau, she lives in two worlds: She is among humans but outside of them. Like Shadow, she learns to embrace her identity and realizes she possesses a human capacity for love. And like Cyan, she is a symbol of extinction: She's the only Esper left by the time it comes to take on Kefka. All of the game's dramatic themes radiate from her. Fittingly, her music is the overworld theme in the World of Balance, a tune that the player will hear over and over for at least half of the game.

Terra lives in two bodies at once—human and Esper—and understands neither. She does not know who she is, and she does not know how to feel. She begins the game as a numb amnesiac, no more than a vessel for magical power; transforms into a luminous wraith, her Esper form; and, as the game's story draws to a close, she settles into her human body and becomes the loving mother to a group of children orphaned in the apocalypse. But her dual identity comes as a surprise to her. She knows she shares an unusual connection with Espers, but she does not learn about her heritage until well into the game. Her first transfiguration, from green-haired human into ghostly purple-white Esper, comes as a shock to the player, to the other heroes, and especially to Terra. She panics, loses control of her body, and streaks across the sky, crashing and destroying and hurtling away again until she collapses from exhaustion. Before she takes flight, she lets out an unforgettable, spine-splitting shriek.

•

Terra's theme does double duty. It describes Terra herself and—because it also serves as the overworld theme for the first half of the game—the world she and the heroes inhabit. The melody begins with little jagged pan-flute peaks rising and falling over a rolling landscape of snare drum, banjo, and electric bass. Strings and horns lay like fog in the valley. This is the grassy wild: the cold wind through the reeds, the banjo pricking like thorns. The frostiness inherent in this first half of the piece isn't just about the environment. When Terra wakes up from her enslavement, her world is cold and lonely—unfamiliar surroundings, uncertain new relationships. She struggles to find warmth and familiarity. She is a stranger in the truest sense of the word: the only human with Esper heritage, the only Esper in the human world.

The theme's second section begins with the rumble of a timpani and clash of a cymbal. The chilly fog disappears; the horns and strings ponder across the plains like shafts of light through the clouds. The meter gallops and the melody flows sun-warmed to the horizon. This is a glance at the second, human half of Terra's story: the trust she builds in her new friends, the peace she makes with herself, and her resolve to fight, borne out of love for her friends and children. This music is two distinct leitmotifs as dual as Terra's body. Cold and warm, Esper and woman, crag and river.

Terra's leitmotifs turn up more often than those of the other playable characters. It appears twice before you even hear her "official" theme (the one labeled "Terra" on the soundtrack). The first instance is in the third section of "Opening Theme," which plays as she and two other soldiers march across the tundra toward the frozen Esper. A gloomy oboe plays the first, Esper-like leitmotif in her theme, and the melody seems mismatched by its setting: A snare drum, electric bass, and, strangely, a harp all stomp out a quick military march. It feels like the oboe is being dragged along against its will. This instance of Terra's theme omits—and nearly all instances that follow omit—the second, warmer, human part. Instead, it ends with the oboe cycling through a series of harrowing harmonies, the harp flicking upward with arpeggio after sharp arpeggio. Finally, the march stutters to a stop and the oboe lands on a sustained, hollow open fifth. Terra is still under the Empire's control here; all this melodic coercion and hopelessness weighs down on us like a musical slave crown.

Terra's theme also makes up the third section in the game's musical overture—the first is the crashing organ, followed by a tinkling piano interlude; the second contains its own, separate (and lengthy) leitmotif associated with catastrophe. These three chunks of music together paint a pretty clear picture of what's to come—they're all central to the game in their own way. Terra's is the only character theme to appear in this overture. This indicates to us that the game we are about to play revolves around this mysterious green-haired soldier and even when it seems not to, it revolves around the ideas and conflicts she represents. This rolls Terra and her theme music both into the overture's heavy-handed foreshadowing; here, her theme is a doom-march.

The second occurrence of this leitmotif, "Awakening," is more dampened than gloomy or ominous. After a hazy introduction by a flute, a piano plays—as in the overture—only the first part of Terra's theme. Between loops, the music blinks its way through an unsteady harp interlude. "Awakening" first plays when Terra's slave crown is removed and she regains consciousness but suffers a severe case of amnesia. The music's bleariness is reflected visually; the graphics move in and out of focus as Terra stumbles out of bed. Terra is disoriented and unsure, and the manipulation of the leitmotif makes us feel it.

"Awakening" also plays at moments of conflict and insight for Terra—each time, she is confronted with some kind of emotional or psychological puzzle. Sometimes her vision is clear and she knows the way; other times the path is murky and she needs guidance. When Terra first transforms into an Esper and disappears, the heroes discuss a plan to find and help her while "Awakening" plays yet again, now indicating Terra's centrality to and presence in the scene, even though she is offscreen—and sketching out the dilemma that all of the characters, including Terra, must now untangle.

Uematsu also breaks Terra's theme up—by more than just lopping off the second leitmotif—and uses the fragments at moments of high drama, especially in the game's first half. During "Save Them!" (figure 4.8), an adrenaline-fueled piece that accompanies the heroes' first major battle against Imperial forces, the first two measures of Terra's theme burst in unexpectedly, shift and stutter slightly, then dive away to safety. This is the fight to protect the frozen Esper—to keep it out of Imperial control—in the very place Terra escaped Imperial control herself. By now, it's been established that Terra has a unique rapport with the creature, and once they drive the Empire away, the heroes hope she can communicate with it to ask for help. Here the quick appearance of the leitmotif further associates Terra with the Espers, and with the rebels' conflict with the Empire. It also reflects the mountains above the tundra, the setting where Terra first appears on screen, and infuses the leitmotif with new meaning: the suggestion of triumph and of the imminence of a crucial moment for Terra. This is just minutes before she first shifts into her body's Esper form.

Figure 4.8 "Save Them!" from Final Fantasy VI, *mm. 22–29 (horn/high strings, melody only). The first leitmotif of Terra's theme can be found in the bracketed sections.*

The same two-measure pattern is in "Metamorphosis," which plays at times of grave danger associated with unchecked magical power: first as the Espers run amok when the sealed barrier to their world is broken, then as Kefka extinguishes the entire race to absorb their power, and then again as the Floating Continent begins its cataclysmic fall to the earth.

This phrase from the first, Esper-like leitmotif crops up again and again. In "Metamorphosis," it's transfigured to trigger the player's fight-or-flight response as it cycles through unsettling diminished harmonies. In the overture, her leitmotif seems to have been associated with calamity, if only by proximity. That relationship becomes almost palpable in "Metamorphosis."

And finally, this mini-leitmotif—chopped down even further and warped almost beyond recognition— also appears as the harp riff that forms the backbone of "Another World of Beasts" (figure 4.9). This track plays in the cave the heroes must pass through as they approach the gate to the Esper world. The melody of the one-measure fragment is stretched like taffy vertically and horizontally, becoming an arpeggio of a diminished seventh chord—a fancy way of saying it sounds weird as heck—but maintaining its same basic contour. It's also modified slightly to accommodate a lopsided septuple meter.

Figure 4.9 "Another World of Beasts" from Final Fantasy VI, *mm. 1–2 (harp).*

All of these recurrences of Terra's theme are drawn only from its first, Esper-ish leitmotif, representing the part of herself she struggles to understand, control, and reconcile. The warmer, more romantic part of her theme is nowhere to be found. Even as Terra embraces motherhood and attempts to abandon her nonhuman side, her Esperhood is ever present—even overly present—and the second leitmotif remains elusive.

During the end-game sequence, that changes. Terra is granted one last conversation with her father, the Esper Maduin. Following Kefka's defeat, magic has begun to disappear from the world—and so have the Espers. And so, for all we know, might Terra. But, as Maduin says to his daughter, if her human half feels a strong attachment to this world, that part of her will continue to live.

This moment, as part of the ending medley, is the first time since the World of Balance—fifteen or twenty hours of gameplay earlier—that we hear that second leitmotif from Terra's theme. Both leitmotifs are played, but this time, the human half comes first, played gently on a flute, accompanied by a harp. The Esper half comes next, now supported by the string section, and goes through a curious set of key changes: from a bittersweet B-flat major to something tangled between B-flat minor and D-flat major, then back to the original B-flat major—this time more tender than it is bittersweet (figure 4.10). It changes from one key into two, then back into one—from sad and alone, then to confused but no longer alone, finally resolving into gladness. The warrior-slave, the powerful wraith, the lost one patting for someone else's hand in the dark—that part of her is laid to rest. All that remains is her humanity, now fully realized in her bond with her friends and her love for her children. For Terra, this end is both cruel and beautiful. It means the death of half of her identity, but it also affirms the wholeness she always sought and believed she would never find.

Figure 4.10 "Ending Theme" from Final Fantasy VI, *mm. 217–229 (flute). Sections "a" and "b" correspond with the first and second leitmotifs of Terra's theme. They are inverted here, so the second motif, "b," comes first.*

Kefka, the Empire, and the Apocalypse

If you look closely during *FF6*'s opening sequence, you will glimpse Kefka's first appearance onscreen—a barely noticeable cameo. He skulks around an empty steel fortress, edging into the bottom right of the frame for a half-second before the camera pans away. There is a lot to feel uneasy about in this opening sequence: the doom-and-gloom history to read on screen, the dreary colors, the ominous music, and a conspicuous lack of plant life. Kefka's quick cameo is another, more subtle reason for unease, and a weighty bit of foreshadowing. He is a stab of color against the bleak, his loud red-and-gold mantle clashing with his nuclear green doublet. His brown hair is pulled back and clipped at one side with a red plume, and he wears a broad ruff the color of spoiled milk. Under each of his eyes is a single red pixel, too red to be blushing skin. Are his irises red? Is he grotesquely made up? Or is he weeping blood?

It's makeup. Kefka is a clown, first and foremost, modeled in the concept art as a Harlequinesque *commedia dell'arte figure*. His first lines of dialogue in the game make him seem buffoonish and pompous, but relatively benign. The first few measures of his theme back this impression up with a sense of cutesy mischief:

plucked strings and oboe bumble around, spinning on their tiptoes like ballerinas about to whack a piñata.

As with Kefka's buffoonery, the musical bumbling doesn't last long. The theme gradually seizes control of itself, growing more sinister with each passing measure. The melody sharpens, pricks, then slashes, like *Psycho*'s Norman Bates taking music therapy. It is so unselfconsciously and violently off-kilter that it is incriminatory. By the time the piece winds down and loops back to the beginning, it has hacked away so much that the inherent humor of the first few measures has capsized into sadistic glee. You hear this glee mirrored by Kefka's signature sound effect: a seven-tone shriek of laughter. With each atrocity he commits, his theme and his laugh are both inculpated, becoming more twisted, heavier, and more disturbing as the game progresses.

The first time you hear Kefka's theme is shortly before the clown himself sets fire to Figaro Castle; you hear it again when he poisons the waters at Doma. The final time this primary version of Kefka's theme plays, he murders General Leo and wipes out the Esper race. This is not a coincidence. This is the point at which Kefka becomes utterly irredeemable, and so does his music. Any pretense of comic relief or lighthearted mischief—or humanity—is excised from his character in this moment, and so goes any silliness in his music.

Kefka's theme is pivotal—in that way, an evil foil to Terra's. As the principal villain, and the only constant character while multitudes of heroes shift in and out of gameplay, Kefka has leitmotifs cropping up left and right, shifting form and meaning depending on when, how, and why they're used. It's textbook leitmotif: evolving as the drama unfolds, adapting to reflect Kefka's fractured mind and his slow theft of Emperor Gestahl's power.

·

Kefka's theme can be broken into four basic motifs. The first is the bumbling, drunken passage on plucked strings (figure 4.11). The second is played first on a flute and oboe and is more intense—as if the first section quit stumbling and suddenly, disturbingly found its footing (figure 4.12). The third is a sudden, violent outburst from the flute, strings, timpani, and cymbal—the first slash of a musical knife (figure 4.13). The fourth and final section is quieter and less obviously sinister, tiptoeing then pirouetting away from the scene of the crime (figure 4.14).

Between the third and fourth motifs, the second repeats itself, now played on the strings and punctuated with the regular crash of a cymbal—a little louder for the people in the back. It was unsettling the first time we heard it—now it's violent. This riff on the strings is a cartoonish reimagining of our *Psycho* shower scene moment, albeit with a shapelier melody. This reiteration doesn't introduce any new material, but is crucial to Kefka's musical portrait: With enough power and a knife to stab with, a disturbed man becomes dangerous.

Figure 4.11 "Kefka," section A, from Final Fantasy VI, *mm. 1–4 (plucked strings).*

Figure 4.12 "Kefka," section B, from Final Fantasy VI, *mm. 7–10 (flute and oboe).*

Figure 4.13 "Kefka," section C, from Final Fantasy VI,
mm. 11 (strings).

Figure 4.14 "Kefka," section D, from Final Fantasy VI,
mm. 17–22 (strings and flute, melody only).

Kefka's story is, in the World of Balance, impossible to untangle from the Empire's. His music, similarly, is tangled up with most of the other evil-related music in the game. Leitmotifs from Kefka's theme become associated with other evil-related leitmotifs, which in turn links them to further evil-related leitmotifs, creating a complicated web of relationships. The first motif, an ascending minor scale that twists its way back down, appears with various fragmentation or variation in "Under Martial Law," (figure 4.15) which plays in Empire-occupied towns, and at the Magitek factory in "Devil's Lab" (figure 3.5). It also appears in a mashed-up, modified form in "Returners," (figure 4.16) the resistance's theme. Here, in the first few measures, the rhythm precisely mirrors the opening measures of Kefka's theme. In fact, this rhythm recurs throughout the Returners' theme, inextricably linking the resistance movement to Kefka himself rather than to the Empire. He is embedded in their music; they may as well have his face on a giant dartboard in their underground headquarters. Though he is ever-present, the Resistance continually rephrases and reshapes their enemy's music, subtly reclaiming it. The group may not succeed in taking Kefka down in the World of Balance, but they're resolved to fight to the end.

Figure 4.15 "Under Martial Law" from Final Fantasy VI, mm. 1–16 (strings and oboe). The bracketed passages "a" and "b" loosely recall the first few measures of Kefka's theme, with its upward minor scale and the twist of eighth-notes that follows. This is also the first instance of the Empire's leitmotif the player hears. (The first eight measures, played on the strings, faintly echo both the Empire's theme and Terra's theme.)

Figure 4.16 "Returners" from Final Fantasy VI, *mm. 5–8 (oboe). The rhythm lines up with Kefka's theme precisely until it lands on the sustained G-sharp. Section "a" is that familiar minor scale, and section "b" follows the same melody that ends the first measure in "Kefka," and also mirrors that first measure's meter—beginning on the final beat and heading into the next measure.*

The Empire, meanwhile, has its own leitmotif, which appears in three places. "The Empire 'Gestahl'" (figure 4.17) plays early in the game, when Kefka torches Figaro Castle in pursuit of Terra (shortly after Kefka's theme occurs for the first time). The player hears this track a few times later in the game, in the Imperial capital and in an abandoned military outpost. "Troops March On" (figure 4.18)—which plays first at an Imperial camp outside Doma, then as Kefka brings a platoon of troops toward the frozen Esper—is essentially an up-tempo version of "Gestahl."

Here's where things get murky. These two Empire themes both start out with a jump of a perfect fifth, leaving some negative space. "Under Martial Law" (see figure 4.15) fills this space with that five-note ascending scale, linking the Empire's leitmotif with Kefka. The opening string riff in "Troops March On" borrows some rhythmic and melodic elements from Kefka's first leitmotif. The musical relationships in these two instances reflect the onscreen relationship between Kefka and the Empire: Though he is technically a high-ranking Imperial leader, their operations are secondary to his personal agenda.

Figure 4.17 "The Empire 'Gestahl'" from Final Fantasy VI, *mm. 9–15 (horn and trumpet, melody only). This melody appears nearly unmodified in "Troops March On," and slightly tweaked in "Under Martial Law."*

Figure 4.18 "Troops March On" from Final Fantasy VI, *mm. 1–4 (strings). The bracketed part strongly resembles the last measure of Kefka's first leitmotif, linking him even more closely to the Empire. Note, however, that we hear this passage of music first, before the Empire's leitmotif is played, suggesting Kefka's primacy.*

•

Finally, a few themes from the game's overture suite are also associated dramatically with Kefka, but unrelated to his theme's leitmotifs. First, the game's opening organ lick—that Jenga tower of perfect fourths that crashes to the ground—appears in the final battle with Kefka as his final form is revealed. That repeated crashing of chords on the pipe organ is echoed in "Fanatics," some creepy musical chaos that plays in an enormous tower built by a cult devoted to Kefka.

Then there's "Catastrophe," a theme associated with the apocalypse. This is first heard during the game's opening cutscene as a short history of the game-world is told on screen—the same cutscene in which Kefka creeps quickly in and out of frame. Later, it appears as its own discrete piece—with a shrill flute leading the melody instead of the low strings from the game's intro—when Kefka murders Gestahl, seizes power, and sets the great cataclysm in motion. You'll hear it just one more time: the opening of the final battle with Kefka.

"Catastrophe" is never heard without Kefka on screen somewhere. As a result of this theme's close association with the character, Kefka becomes a metonym for the end of the world.

Finally, there is "Dancing Mad," the four-movement accompaniment to this final battle. "Dancing Mad" is a prog rock mashup of all Kefka-related motifs, minus any obviously recognizable as the now-defunct Empire's. All four movements are full of variations on fragments from Kefka's theme, divided or interspersed with "Catastrophe" and the hubristic Jenga-organ, culminating in a menacing, jagged rock anthem. The whole suite—like Kefka's new godlike form—is at once recognizably him and also something new, enormous, and terrifying.

MARIA AND DRACO

"I DIDN'T REALLY WORRY ABOUT IT," Nobuo Uematsu told me when I asked him if he was concerned about the way his in-game opera would be received. If I imagine myself in his position, with only my entry-level college music theory and composition under my belt—more formal training than the composer himself—I develop Yasunori Mitsuda–style stomach ulcers. Even if I had Uematsu's talent as a composer, and I'd grown comfortable scoring big-name video games, I would have had reservations about including an opera—especially in 90s America, where video games were "for boys" and classical music was "for sissies" (or weirdos). My compositions would have needed to be strong and skillful enough to jump over a mile-high cultural hurdle. If the game were considered a stateside flop—if boys weren't buying it here—that could have meant the end of a popular franchise in America, and a major loss of revenue for my employer. My opera could have been cited in the history books as a true what-not-to-wear moment. The Atari's

E.T. the Extra-Terrestrial of video game scores. As far as I'm concerned, Uematsu had nerves of steel—the idea of failure never even occurred to him.

In America, gender certainly factored into the reception of *Final Fantasy VI*. It was designed to. The game's marketing doubled down on masculinity—in hindsight, it seems almost desperate. In a TV spot, a claymation Moogle—an adorable little white bear-bat, and an unofficial mascot of the Final Fantasy series—sits behind a casting desk, cracks wise with a Danny DeVito–like voice, and uses lightning bolts to zap a steady stream of auditioning monsters. At the end of the commercial, a narrator asks: "*Final Fantasy III*: Do you have what it takes?" He is accompanied by a totally sweet electric guitar riff. Cowabunga, dudes.

At the back of *Nintendo Power's* magazine-length strategy guide for the game, a catalogue offered a healthy selection of merch, including a *Final Fantasy III*-branded Hanes Beefy-T, emblazoned thus: "NO WIMPS." A Moogle appears in front of the text, leaning jauntily on an oversized dagger. On a second t-shirt, a horde of bright-colored monsters occupies the top half and the same dagger-leaning Moogle appears at the bottom, along with the text: "*Final Fantasy III*: The Ultimate Fantasy." Also included in the catalogue: a wristwatch, a baseball cap, and a poster, all with the same dagger-Moogle art. The poster—which includes the same large, bright horde of monsters found on one of the t-shirts—asks, "It doesn't seem fair, does it?" A companion ad shows the monsters reduced to piles of bone and ash. Our Moogle smugly asks, "Who says life is fair?" Copy at the bottom of the ad tells you this game will "blow you out of your shorts." There are a lot of Freudian implications to puzzle out, but the power fantasy is clear: Kick some ass! Torch some monsters! Compensate for something!

In addition to virtually every promo and every piece of swag, the Moogle-with-dagger image appears on the game's box art, the cover of the game's manual, and the cover of the American print of the soundtrack, titled *Kefka's Domain*. The image is absent from Japanese ads, as well as the game's Japanese box art, which features a melancholy illustration of Terra, mounted in—or poised to leap from—her robotic Magitek armor, gazing from afar at a lofty cityscape. The Japanese illustration promises darkness, strangeness, and exploration—not machismo. The Japanese soundtrack release simply has the game's logo on a white background, labeled *Final Fantasy VI: Original Sound Version*. There's no "domain"—no connotation of ownership, power, or invasion.

Nowhere in Yoshitaka Amano's concept art do Moogles appear wielding any kind of weapon; they mostly wave hello, waddle, hop, tumble, and sleep like drunk pandas. The dagger-Moogle is an American invention, or it was invented for America, a nation of cool dudes who, despite their coolness, needed reassurance that ass-kicking would be a primary feature of the game. This image manages to use an adorable little cuddle-bear in a direct appeal to macho (or macho-aspiring) gamers who blow off steam through fantasy violence—gamers whose inclinations lean more toward *Mortal Kombat* or *Street Fighter II* than, say, Hello Kitty. It's kawaii repackaged for the JV football team.

•

FF6, though it isn't short of gender problems, centers two of the female heroes—Terra and Celes—by giving them more to do than all of their male counterparts. The plot in the World of Balance revolves around Terra, and in the World of Ruin, Celes is the de facto captain of the *D2: The Mighty Ducks*–style recruitment effort. The game's US marketing does nothing to suggest the primacy (or even presence) of two women protagonists. Square minimized the game's emotional and romantic content by emphasizing toughness, cartoon violence, and roughhousing humor in its marketing materials. The company signaled to young boys that they would see their ideal versions of themselves reflected in the game. Boys could play without dinging their fragile masculinity, even if—ew—things got a little emotional.

The ads don't just feel hypermasculine (and exclusionary to sissies and weirdos like yours truly), they are outright misrepresentations of the game. Beyond its two central heroines, it's got love stories, loss stories, soapy plot twists, and parent-child bonding. In-game violence is abstracted: Characters mime their attacks at a safe distance from enemies and corporeal damage is represented by numbers, not blood. There's no Hulk-smashing or puffed-chest posturing. The game explores a broken world and characters with broken lives. Truly, nothing about *FF6* is butch, at least not in the American sense. But conventional marketing wisdom was to target budding gamer-bros who would respond to appeals to their violent dudeliness rather than their emotion or intellect.

With truly pyrotechnic irony, the game's most famous sequence is a stirring, swords-sheathed opera. American marketers couldn't have known that this scene would become the monument it is today—but even if they had, they would not have dared to market the game based on it. If you sit through three episodes of the popular 90s sitcom *Home Improvement*, you will have absorbed the idea that opera is a snoozefest designed for femmes and borings, not for football-havers.

So it surprised me that my non-sissy, non-weirdo male peers reacted to the in-game opera not with dread or dismissal, but with deep affection—as they did for the rest of the game's squishiness. Maybe it was digestible to them because the opera wasn't three hours long, or because it was during a video game and not a field trip or forced outing, or because the music is a bit easier to interpret than that of real-world operas. Still, three hours long or twelve minutes long. It's called an opera. And a generation of boys did more than suffer through the perceived femininity, social toxicity, and emasculation of a welling-up tear. They adored it—and still do.

In his book *Sound Play*, musicologist William Cheng points out that YouTube recordings of the opera scene—just recordings of the scene itself, ripped straight from the game, presented without comment or reinterpretation—are surprisingly popular. They rack up tens or hundreds of thousands of views apiece, and attract flocks of emotional commenters (of all genders) who confess goosebumps and weepiness. One YouTube user, first name "Jock," comments: "This lingers, this touches even today. Wow." Another, "Mikey," says, "I'm not crying! I just so happen to chopped [*sic*] onions while watching this." And someone called "The Ninjapartyman" sums it up most concisely: "i cri evry tim."

Kill the Wabbit

The strings tune to a concert A. The brass section warms up. The audience members flip through their programs, and the show begins. Rolling thunder. Flashes of lighting. The hero appears, announcing he is on the hunt. He wanders hither and yon, tracking his prey.

Wearing a gold-plated soup can and coordinating horned helmet, Elmer Fudd repeatedly warbles: "Kill the wabbit!" Bugs Bunny enters slyly, stage left. Comedy ensues. Bugs evades capture by dressing in full drag, serving Rhinemaiden realness (or, more accurately, Valkyrie verisimilitude). Fudd falls in love with the beguiling doe, drag name Brünnhilde. But when the two go in for the kiss, the shield-maiden's wig gets snatched. Fudd rages, using his magic helmet to rend the sky and cast a mountain down on the luckless lapin, now gone limp. When he realizes what he has done, he is tortured with guilt. He gathers the rabbit's body and marches it toward Valhalla.

Before the curtains are drawn, Bugs lifts his head and addresses the audience: "What did you expect in an opera? A happy ending?"

This is "What's Opera, Doc?", the iconic 1957 cartoon short. It quotes, with sumptuous irony, the music of the widely celebrated and wildly self-serious Richard Wagner, whose *Ring Cycle* (*Der Ring des Nibelungen*, famous for its use of leitmotif) is everything fans love about opera—and everything that everyone else hates. The cartoon's insane mélange of comedic and dramatic tropes fantastically sends up opera—but the mishmash, ironically and appropriately, makes the cartoon itself genuinely operatic. The dramatic is gift-wrapped in the comedic, just as *FF6*'s mushiness was veiled in masculinity. "What's Opera Doc?" has all the hallmarks of the subject it's satirizing: a blustering villain, a clever hero, supernatural forces, disguise, comedy, love, rage, murder, remorse, redemption. "What's Opera, Doc?" answers its own question. This *is* opera, doc.

•

Like "What's Opera, Doc?", *FF6* approaches opera with layers of irony, though with wholly different intent. In the cartoon, the opera itself is the farce, played straight for the viewer. In the game, the opera is sincerely dramatic—but, through no fault of its own, ends in farce.

This is because we have two operas happening at the same time: one onstage and one off. Offstage, the gambler Setzer has just sent a letter to the famous diva, Maria, politely notifying her in advance of his plans to kidnap her during an upcoming performance. The heroes come across the note and see an opportunity: They need access to Setzer's airship to continue their fight against the empire, and now they know where and when to find him. In a stroke of magnificent luck, Celes—the former Imperial general—is a dead ringer for the diva, and coincidentally happens to be a pretty good singer. The heroes plan to plant Celes in the opera house so that, when Setzer whisks her away, they can hijack his airship. Two schemes, scheming against each other at the same time. What could possibly go wrong?

Well, this can go wrong: When the player arrives at the opera house, Ultros, a sass-blasting purple octopus—whom the heroes soundly whopped earlier in the game—shows up just as the whole operation is about to begin. Furious with the heroes for having humiliated him in their previous encounter, he leaves his own note politely notifying the heroes in advance that he is planning his own, entirely separate scheme. "I owe you one," it reads, "So I'm gonna jam up your opera!"

The plot of the onstage opera is simple enough: The West's great hero Draco is out to war, pining for his love Maria (Celes), who is a hostage of the East—and the two are on course to be reunited one way or another. For those keeping count, we're now up to three simultaneous offstage schemes. The opera, that pesky fully orchestrated stage performance, is only getting in the way—and it's certainly not going to end as planned.

After the overture, Draco enters stage left for the show's first, dramatic scene: Alone on the battlefield, he is trampled by a herd of Chocobos—those marshmallow ostriches typically mounted by humans for transit. He pulls himself up from the ground to sing his love for Maria. In the next scene, Maria—who is set to be married to the enemy Prince Ralse of the East—sings of her love for Draco. In the third scene, a celebratory ball, Prince Ralse forces Maria into a pre-wedding dance—until the party is crashed by the hero Draco, now mounted on a Chocobo of his own, trampling the revelers in a nice dramatic parallel. A fight breaks out between Draco and Ralse, between the survivors of the West and the occupiers of the East. If the opera were to proceed as planned, it would likely resolve in one of two ways: Prince Ralse would be defeated and Draco and Maria would be happily reunited, or—and this seems by far the more likely option—Draco would be killed and Maria would have a juicy mad scene (an operatic performance of insanity) before murdering Ralse on their wedding night.

•

At the end of the opera's first scene, Locke heads backstage to catch Celes before her big aria. He arrives in her dressing room to see she has changed out of her armor into a cream-colored gown; her hair, usually worn long and held back at the sides with barrettes, is elaborately done up and intertwined with a midnight-blue ribbon that sets off a few periwinkle accents on her gown. Locke blushes—definitively showing, for the first time, his true feelings for Celes. "That ribbon suits you," is all Locke can stammer. Celes takes one last look at her score and heads onstage.

Celes's aria is the jewel of *FF6*. It's lovely, sensitively directed, and it obliquely indicates that Celes might reciprocate Locke's feelings—a surprise to the player. In fact, the aria itself comes as a bit of a surprise; though you can read the lyrics before heading onstage, you have no clue what it's going to sound like.

It starts out sweet and simple, set just for the soprano and a serene music box–like pattern on the harp—suggesting, as the words do, upwelling memories. Celes wanders slowly through the loggia of a castle, stopping every now and then to lean toward the balustrade and sing. "Must I forget you? Our solemn promise? Will autumn take the place of spring? What shall I do? I'm lost without you. Speak to me once more!" She doubts she will ever see Draco again, but swears her fidelity, believing—or trying to convince herself—that eventually he'll return. This is a 16-bit equivalent of Cio-Cio-san's "Un bel dì, vedremo" (Puccini's *Madame Butterfly*, 1904) or Rusalka's "Song to the Moon" (Dvořák's *Rusalka*, 1901). In both well-loved arias, the tragic heroine awaits her love against the impossible.

Note the way Maria's story mirrors Locke's: an absent beloved, presumed dead by the hand of an enemy force; a refusal to let go; a slim hope that the beloved will return someday and that everything will be set right.

A ghostly Draco appears onstage toward the end of Maria's aria, and she takes a break from singing to dance with the specter of her love. He laughs with her one last time, then disappears. Through the magic of theatre, he transforms into a bouquet of roses. (How a real-life opera company would pull this off, I don't know, but I'd like to speak to the production staff that could.) Maria picks up the flowers, heads to the castle's balcony and sings the aria's last line, "I'll wait for you always." She tosses the flowers to the sky; they arc gently upward then fall, in slow motion, to the ground far below.

Later in the game, if Celes loses hope after she wakes up in the World of Ruin (that is, if father-figure Cid dies) she will attempt suicide. Before her attempt, her theme music—an orchestrated version of this aria—begins to play. She climbs to the top of a mountain, where a cliff faces the sea. She thinks of Locke, who, like Draco, seems to have vanished from her life forever. Then she jumps toward the rocks below, arcing outward and down in slow motion, just as Maria's bouquet of roses.

•

In our offstage opera, Ultros has devised a plan to drop a four-ton weight from the rafters onto the performers below. He might as well be Wile E. Coyote with an Acme-brand anvil—a true "What's Opera, Doc?" moment. The heroes notice him in the rafters after Celes's aria, just as Draco heroically rides onstage. They must stop this mad cephalopod. Losing Celes would be a tragedy, and it would nullify their entire ruse. If she's flattened into a blood pancake, there is no diva for the wealthy Setzer to abduct. Two operas foiled by a triumphant purple octopus.

The heroes race through the catwalks and, after a scuffle, they crash onto the stage, Ultros in tow—the anvil, fortunately, stays put. This interrupts the opera's climax but miraculously causes no injuries. The audience begins to murmur in confusion. The impresario steps onstage, desperate to save his own opera, and insists hysterically that the show go on. Locke clumsily introduces himself to the audience as "the world's premiere adventurer," arrived from on high to save the distressed Maria. Ultros steps in to insult Locke's parentage, then attacks. The orchestra takes the cue and strikes up some high-energy accompaniment as the players formally battle the octopus, concluding Ultros's opera just as it collides with the stage's.

Let's pause for a moment to recognize another operatic trope in this mashup of conflicting dramas: the love triangle. It's nearly a love polyhedron: Draco and Maria love each other, and jealous Ralse loves Maria; Setzer is into Celes, but only as Maria; and though Locke and

Celes are mutually attracted to each other, Locke is still hung up on his dead fiancée Rachel (whom, at this point in the game, he is still hoping to resuscitate). It may be best not to speculate on whether or not Ultros has any romantic motives here.

Celes's aria is not the only element that makes this scene a hit. The music is memorable, yes. But this passage of the game has disguises, drama-within-a-drama-within-a-drama, plot twists, complicated romances, slapstick, live animals, the breaking of the fourth wall, memorable characters, sword-fighting, sets, the impossible stagecraft of a knight-turned-bouquet and a talking purple octopus, and a flawlessly improvising orchestra. I'd pay good money to see it at the Met.

One way or another, this was all going to be ground to a halt by Setzer—and indeed, he shows up just after Ultros has been walloped anew. The stylish, gray-haired gambler interrupts the interruption, swoops in, and whisks Celes away. He's a supporting character, a hero, and an antihero. He's a means to an end in *The Returners vs. the Empire*, the hero of the opera playing in his head, and a villainous kidnapper in *Maria and Draco*.

As the gambler and soprano exit the theatre through unknown means and the other heroes scramble after them, the stage performance ends (with the frenzied impresario selling the audience on an exciting sequel, to be performed at a date to be announced). But the next act in the offstage opera—that scheme to nab Setzer's airship—takes off.

A Tale of Two Operas

Ryan Thompson's theory that *FF6* is, in itself, an opera goes far beyond the three-act structure he cites as evidence. He also notes the game's large cast of characters and its built-in *dramatis personae* to help spectators identify them: When each character is introduced, they receive a few short lines of description, as might appear at the beginning of an opera score ("Figaro, the count's valet," "Susanna, the countess's maid," "Locke: Treasure hunter and trail-worn traveler, searching the world over for relics of the past…"). The game's ending sequence is a kind of curtain call. In addition to giving each character a short coda to tie a bow on their story, it credits each of them as though they have been played by actors ("CELES as Celes Chere"). As mentioned earlier, each human character (with the exception of Gau, Shadow, and the maybe-human Gogo) is given a European-sounding surname, giving the impression that you may be reading the cast list on the back of a dusty box-set recording. (Like older Hollywood films, older opera recordings tended to have homogeneously white European or American casts.) *FF6*'s in-game opera is about two warring entities and the woman caught in the middle—vaguely reflecting the plot of the game and reinforcing the suggestion of game as opera.

Both Uematsu and the game's writers (who could well have been as new to opera as Uematsu) did a pretty good job creating a structurally operatic game in spite of themselves. Outside of the opera sequence, and the parallelisms between game and opera, a few references to opera are planted here and there: Figaro castle, Mozart's *The Marriage of Figaro*; the swordsman Ziegfried, as in Wagner's *Siegfried*; and Celes impersonating the diva Maria—perhaps a nod to the legendary Maria Callas. Two items—a scratched opera record and an opera singer's autograph—are embedded in the game's code but do not appear in the final version of the game. Turn-of-the-century phonographs are scattered in houses and business establishments throughout the game. Given that real-world phonographs predate pop music as we know it, and given the scratched record embedded in the game's code, it's not crazy to infer that the developers envisioned the game's citizenry listening to classical opera for leisure.

The game is also rife with other operatic tropes. It has poisoning, as at Doma. There are suicides, as Celes attempts if Cid dies on the deserted island, and as Shadow commits at the end of the game. An execution looms, as Celes's does before Locke frees her. Damsels are in distress, as all three female playable characters are at one point or another. There are betrayals and backstabbings: The Empire betrays the Returners after a peace accord; Kefka stabs General Leo; Celes stabs Kefka; and Kefka betrays, then physically stabs, Gestahl on the Floating Continent. Flimsy disguises are another operatic trope: In addition to Celes as Maria, Edgar disguises himself as a gang leader named Gerad, and Locke steals and dons clothing from merchants and soldiers to sneak around an Empire-occupied town. (Shadow and Gogo are in disguise the entire game.) Kefka's presence is one protracted mad scene—called out explicitly in the final Kefka-related music, "Dancing Mad." In concept art, Kefka is depicted as a clown; not only is the history of opera tangled up with the earliest roots of modern clowning, but the idea of a mad clown is the actual plot of Leoncavallo's *Pagliacci* (1892). This one is famous for its aria "Vesti la giubba"—one of those pieces you'll know when you hear—sung by the lead character, a clown named Canio.

Canio, by the way—big on stabbing.

If we run with Thompson's idea and think of *FF6* as a self-contained opera, that makes the game's opera scene an opera within an opera. *Pagliacci* is almost that: a *commedia dell'arte* performance interrupted with Canio viciously stabbing his lover. *FF6*'s opera within an opera is interwoven with comedic antics (operatic in themselves)—as the heroes step away from their seats and go on a madcap chase to find Ultros and his four-ton weight. This head-spinning meta-commentary may make *Ariadne auf Naxos* (Richard Strauss, 1912–1916) a closer analogue than *Pagliacci*; in *Ariadne*, a wealthy patron commissions a dramatic opera, whose performance is crashed by a bunch of (non-violent, genuinely comedic) clowns.

Uematsu's score for *FF6* also has several qualities in common with opera beyond its use of leitmotif. It plays an outsize role in selling the story and characters to the audience. At several points, the music is written and cued in such a way that it lines up with cutscenes. The best examples of this are the prologue, the opera, and the end credits, though many other moments also have well-timed cues. It's also orchestrated like an opera, in that you'd find most of the score's instruments in an orchestra pit. Maybe a 20th-century pit—one that has a few synthesizers and an electric bass lying around.

Ariadne auf Naxos, whose dramatic opera-within-an-opera is threatened with comedic ruin, commented on the intersection of "high art" and "low art," as well as the intersection of art and commerce. In *Ariadne*, a composer and a small cohort of singers are horrified when they find out that their dramatic opera will be performed with the help of a troupe of clowns—at the insistence of the patron funding their show. The self-serious and egotistical "high-brow" performers are forced to confront a bald reality: that the performance of their opera hinges on the whim of a single wealthy backer. The clowns, though, are more than happy to make light of the opera, and have no problem with a little flexibility as long as they'll still get paid. The characters in the opera do not comment on the performance once it's finished, but the show reaches a satisfying conclusion and the drama was made richer for the clowns' presence. At first a commercial flop in 1912, *Ariadne* became a fan favorite after a successful 1916 revision, which is still commonly performed today—more than a hundred years after its premiere.

FF6's opera sequence does the same high-low, art-commerce schtick. The opera house's impresario is initially woebegone when Ultros and the game's heroes fall from the rafters and crash his show. But he realizes, once he gets over Locke's terrible acting, that the audience is eating it up. He quickly turns the unexpected events to his favor, encouraging the audience to return another night for the exciting conclusion—which is to say, he's willing to toss away high art once he realizes he can turn a profit with slapstick. Writ large, *FF6* is an ambitious, dramatic story with a rich, innovative score (high-brow) packaged in a video game (low-brow)—a medium whose legitimacy as "real art" had not seriously been considered in 1994. This was a story that needed to be told as much as a product that needed to be sold. "NO WIMPS," remember? The game as a story, and the cartridge as a product, comment on the same matrix of conflicting ideas and interests as *Ariadne*.

In its bones, *FF6* has the marrow of a centuries-old tradition of storytelling—a seven-layer dip of comedy, drama, sincerity, irony, music, visuals, and writing. *FF6* doesn't pose the existential question "What's a video game?"—but it certainly answers it. *This* is a video game, doc.

•

This evening at the opera ends up being more than a diversion; it serves some important dramatic functions. It introduces Celes's theme music which, unlike the other characters', does not play when she is introduced. It inches the plot forward. It provides a moment of character development for Celes (and, to a lesser extent, Setzer and Locke). It intensifies Celes's relationship with Locke and infuses her potential suicide attempt with extra meaning. It adds memorable detail to the game-world.

The opera sequence also creates a powerful musical memory: The heartbreak of this aria is inextricable from each subsequent recurrence of Celes's theme. But it also serves a radical aesthetic function for a video game of this era. It isn't simply music under a cutscene, and it isn't simply diegetic music. It's a concert—free tickets with every game—uniquely wrapping up all of the above.

There are far less circuitous ways to get characters from hither to yon—ways that don't involve doppelgängers, highly unlikely hidden talents, kidnappings, and octopus B-stories. The party could simply have run into Setzer somewhere else without appreciably changing his character or the game's plot. He is a wealthy gambler, so the party could have gotten into a bidding war with him at the game's auction house (which auctions off, among some genuinely valuable items, a 1/1200 scale model of the very airship the heroes try to steal). Wherever the encounter were to happen, Setzer still could have been taken with a famous singer named Maria and Celes still could have posed as her to trick him—no performing involved. Or it could have played out differently. Maybe Celes could have reminded Setzer of his lost love, Daryl, and she used that to her advantage. Maybe Setzer and Locke could have competed for Celes's affection, and Locke would feign backing off to convince Setzer to fly them south. There are also ways this could have worked without objectifying Celes. For instance, if the party just bumped into Setzer on the street and he was nice.

So why on earth go to the opera?

EarthBound, released in Japan about four months after *FF6*, features a Blues Brothers–like band called the Runaway Five; helping the band (and watching them play a set) is a required part of the game. In many respects, this sequence is similar to *FF6*'s opera—though it strikes me as a much less risky move. Opera was (and is) a cliché pop-culture punchline; blues was not. And even though blues wasn't the most common sound for contemporary pop music in the 90s, its gritty coolness granted it understandable appeal (or at least palatability) even among hip, cool teens. At the very least, blues is much closer to pop in the musical phylogeny than opera is, and for that proximity it carries much less stigma. For *FF6*'s developers, the less risky option would have been to omit the opera entirely.

It is the game creators' job, and in their best interest, to keep players immersed in the game-world. Using opera—if not with accuracy, then at least with respect—posed an extreme risk: It could distract, bore, repel, or easily backfire into complete self-parody (some self-parody is intentionally woven in, providing some risk-mitigation). The story of Maria and Draco in *FF6* does not do any of these things, despite leaning into operatic tropes. Instead of rejecting the scene, gamers have rallied around it, cementing it as an important, revered moment in game history.

Broadly held cultural notions about opera as highly intellectual and inaccessibly beautiful may contribute to the scene's aesthetic success by leading the player to believe that something extraordinary is about to happen. That is, the expectation that the opera scene will be extraordinary may be exactly what makes it extraordinary. We believe we are going to witness something transcendent and, as a result, we do.

Even without the music, the scene carries dramatic heft. Locke's and Celes's feelings begin to bubble closer to the surface. Celes wears her evening gown only once during the game, and it's here. For a 16-bit game, a one-shot, total costume change is a big deal, usually indicating a scene or moment's significance. (Another example of this is Gau's dressing up to meet his father.) Then there are the stunning visuals: Celes singing her aria by the light of the moon and stars, wending through a set with a tremendous sense of scale; the dance with the ghostly knight; the roses sweeping past the waxing moon. The scene in itself addresses the characters' emotions obviously but indirectly, and the sequence is (minimally) interactive, forcing closer observation by the player. All of these non-musical elements amplify the opera's impact.

In times of tragedy, art helps us preserve our humanity, recording it and reminding us of it. Even before the apocalypse, the world of *FF6* is riddled with war and suffering. I like to think that, in the game-world, the composer of Maria and Draco's opera knew this. This story—about war and occupation, about men robbing women of their agency—touches on, or arises from, the oppression experienced by the game-world's peoples. Loss, resignation, resoluteness, the ebb and flow of hope: These are experiences shared by each of the game's main characters, by the nameless citizens in occupied territory, by the survivors of Narshe and Doma, by the disappearing Espers. Even faceless Imperial stormtroopers, in their complicity, have lost a part of themselves.

Art recovers what oppression steals; it is survival and resistance. The more dire our circumstances, the more necessary it becomes. In the grey-brown landscape of the World of Ruin, that memory of that night at the opera still glitters. It may well be that, through the horror of the apocalypse, the memory of this night at the opera—or other nights like it—is what keeps the world breathing.

•

A quick Google search of "'final fantasy 6' 'opera'" will return a healthy smattering of results that include recaps, reviews, playthroughs, analyses, personal essays, fan art, performances, remixes, forum threads, and Q&As. You will see the word "goosebumps" bandied about so much that it will begin to lose its meaning. (It's rare to encounter a post from a person online who didn't find the sequence stirring, though there certainly are a few.) In recent years, the game and its opera have even begun to receive academic attention. The field of ludomusicology is gaining steam in a way it certainly was not in the mid-90s. I don't think this is a coincidence; scholar-musicians entering academia in the past twenty years came of age with the SNES, and their skin probably prickled, as mine did, when Celes first took to the stage.

I pursued opera singing, as a student and professional, for over ten years, and even my experience with and knowledge of the real-live art form hasn't turned me off of this 16-bit facsimile. I'm self-aware enough to admit that my experience with this game influenced my choice to study classical singing. I can trace my attraction to opera back well before I stumbled on Mozart's *Die Zauberflöte* (*The Magic Flute*, 1791) as a high-school senior—it began in fifth grade, when I stumbled my way through *Maria and Draco*.

William Cheng attributes the emotional appeal of the opera scene, in part, to semiotics. Remember the Mario Pit? We learn to love the little chibi-nuggets as though they're our own friends. That's semiotics—we take a video game's graphics in as a visual signal, and we interpret what those signals mean: a person, a coin, an octopus, a treasure chest. We recognize that they're not real people or treasure chests, but we imagine them as their real-life counterparts. Our mind fills in the blanks for us. And the more it does that, the more the line blurs between our lived reality and the game's signaled reality—the more immersed we are.

We fill in the audio blanks as much as the graphical ones. When we hear a string section playing in any of *FF6*'s music, we are not hearing actual strings—or even faithful recordings of actual strings. What we're hearing is the best approximation (accounting for style) that the game can give us: a sound sample, pitched high or low, that carries just enough aural markers so that when we hear it, we think, "That's supposed to be a string section!"

Cheng takes this analysis and applies it to Celes's human singing voice. One of the things that makes it so affecting is that we are trained by hours of chibi context to interpret it as human whether or not it really sounds that way—and, to be clear: It doesn't.

FF6's opera voices are actual recordings of people singing, but storage capacity on SNES cartridges necessitated compromise in audio quality. The voice samples are stretched to their limits: They're compressed to a relatively low quality, and they further lose fidelity as the SNES hardware manipulates the samples up and down the scale. The voices' vibrato pulses quicken the higher up they go, and slow down the lower they go. (This applies to all of the instrument samples, not just the operatic voices—but because vibrato is such an important part of a singing voice, it is especially noticeable in this situation.)

Vibrato is one good heuristic for judging a real-world classical singer's performance: If the voice pulses quickly and evenly up and down the singer's range, you can generally infer their technique is good; if it slows down, speeds up, or unintentionally disappears, they likely have some more learning or practicing to do. And if it's a slow, wide wobble all the way through, you can chalk it up to persistent bad habits. Because of the way the SNES stretches and shrinks and its virtual instruments, the voices—Celes's especially—don't pass muster by this metric.

Celes's aria is not exactly virtuosic. It's just one octave, from D4 to D5, with a low enough tessitura that any elderly alto from any volunteer church choir would have no trouble singing along beautifully. But the SNES's technological limitations sometimes makes the aria sound like a struggle. When it descends to that low D, the vibrato pulse in Celes's synthesized voice slows to a ponderous warble. It sounds healthier in its middle and upper ranges—but if she sang much higher than D5, you could expect a sound like Alvin and the Chipmunks.

Beyond this, the voices do not move between notes in the same way that a human voice would; they step up and down like robots, starting and stopping the sound each time. A skilled singer would likely sing this piece as one nice legato line—think a single, bright, unbroken filament that runs through and between each note. They would only slice through this filament for a well-timed breath, or as part of an intentional interpretive choice.

Robo-stepping, though, is generally not an intentional interpretive choice. It's another cardinal sin in classical singing—a good sense of line is crucial.

Celes doesn't actually sing any words, which is fine; it can be lovely to listen to a nice vocalise. The trouble is that she doesn't even sing any recognizable vowel sounds, and whatever made-up vowel she's singing seems to shift with the pitch just as her vibrato does. The best way to imitate her sound might be to sing both sounds in the word "or" simultaneously. Or is it more of a "war?" Or a "waw?"

The problems with Celes's voice—as with Draco's and Ralse's—are steep and multitudinous. If they were real voices attached to real people, and those people stepped into a vocal studio, their teacher would take an early retirement right there on the spot.

But that's not really the point of listening to Celes sing, is it? Knowing all this, being able to evaluate Celes's "voice" in the abstract, doesn't affect our enjoyment of it.

•

In "One-Winged Angel," Sephiroth's theme from *FF7*—which came out only three years after *FF6*—Uematsu was able to include a recorded chorus of voices that recognizably sings words from the *Carmina Burana*, a group of medieval secular Latin poems best known for being set to music by Carl Orff. He would have done the same in *FF6* if he could have. When I asked him about what went into choosing sound samples for the game, he said he worked with sound programmers to create better-sounding virtual instruments for each successive game. "I'd choose sound sources that wouldn't lose their individuality even if they were deformed for inclusion in the game," he told me. Uematsu was a master of circumventing the limits of whatever hardware he happened to be working with— but found the technological constraints on his music dissatisfying, even with "One-Winged Angel." In a 2014 interview with Red Bull Music Academy Daily, he said *Final Fantasy VIII* (1999) was "[t]he first time I was able to have the kind of orchestral music I wanted. [...] For the opening and ending, I actually got an orchestra and choir involved, and was able to record them live."

But if, for *FF6*'s opera, he could have had live-recorded, high-fidelity recordings of singers and orchestra, would it have been a good idea to use them? I say no.

The fact that the synthesized voices in *FF6* are fairly poor representations of their real-world counterparts may actually work in the game's favor. In the case of "One-Winged Angel," the singing occurs as part of an epic, but still obviously synthesized, orchestration. The vocals aren't as naked in "Angel" as they are in the opera scene; if they were, the listener would hear clear human voices on top of synthesized instruments, which would be distracting—drawing attention out of the game to reconcile the live with the synthesized. The recording of the chorus of "Angel," when isolated from its accompaniment, is of clearly low quality, with audible compression artifacts. Compressed audio is economical for storage space, but it also makes the voices sound almost computerized in places—awkward on their own, but fitting with the rest of the game's synthesized instruments. The overall effect is truer to life than Celes's aria, but then, so were *FF7*'s visuals—blocky masses of polygons, yes, but a step forward in the march of gaming technology.

"One-Winged Angel" is non-diegetic, meaning that the characters aren't supposed to be able to hear it and that it isn't coming from a source within the game's fictional world. It's just for the player. Because of this, we're not bringing the same set of expectations to our listening as we might if a group of characters was singing it onscreen for us to hear. If we were, we'd want the voices to sound the way the characters look: flatter and chunkier than real life.

The realness of Celes's voice is proportional to her appearance. It sounds as much like a human voice as Celes's white-dressed character sprite looks like a real-life opera diva. Which is to say, we are listening to a pixelated treasure chest. We know it's not real, but we hear it as such because of its context—that's our brain filling in the blanks. A truer or falser voice might jar us out of our semiotic groove, calling attention to itself as more or less real than other elements of the game—and thereby shattering the dramatic illusion in which we've chosen to immerse ourselves.

•

Many people find opera unlistenable, having precisely the same reaction I do when I hear Ed Sheeran. I get it. Operatic voices, for many, are like olives: a developed taste. These are voices trained to accomplish the superhuman feat of being understood clearly over a full orchestra, almost always without artificial amplification. As a result, they're muscular and proportioned in a way that pop singers' voices aren't. They sound alien—even absurd—if you're not used to them. And if it's not the voices, it's classical music in general. It can feel out-of-reach, self-serious, intimidating, or boring.

But by the time we hear Celes's aria, we've been listening to synthesized semi-classical, semi-prog rock music for many hours, we've been looking at pixelated representations of humans, and we've been exploring a preprogrammed steampunk world. We don't interpret Celes's voice the way we would a human singer's; instead, we interpret it within the semiotic framework the game has been building. We understand the voice to be beautiful because it's heard as beautiful in the game-world—even if it's deeply flawed or ugly on its face, even if the player finds real-world opera a total drag.

Nothing makes me more aware of this phenomenon than when I hear live orchestras and singers performing video game music—especially Celes's aria. I've listened to a number of recordings of "Aria de Mezzo Carattere" performed by a real singer and orchestra a number of times, but I'll admit I can never sit all the way through them. When I listen to a live singer and orchestra, that semiotic illusion I have baked into my brain disappears and I hear the music, and judge it, as I would any other kind of music. I begin to notice flaws in the singer's voice, question the music's orchestration, and consider its schmaltz. It unsettles me in a way I can't quite move past—sort of the inverse of the Mario Gap, the equivalent of seeing Sonic the Hedgehog's disturbing CGI presence in the early previews of his eponymous 2020 film.

I have no such worries when Celes sings in glorious 16-bit sound. I am blissfully in the moment and I perceive her strange, robotic performance for what it is meant to be: an emotionally charged aria, sparkling bright as far back as the cheap seats in the living room, a surprising show of vulnerability from a person I'm having a hard time getting to know, a strange aesthetic diversion from, and reflection of and on a world in shambles.

NOSTALGITEK FACTORY

MUSIC CAN HELP US NAVIGATE and survive the social Thunderdome we call adolescence, determining in part who our friends are, how we interact with the world, and how we begin to carve out our adult identities. The growing independence that comes with our ascent to adulthood means we can increasingly forage for our own music and define our own tastes. We're influenced by the listening habits of our friends and frenemies, fitting in or trying to stand out by bucking trends. Our musical affinities might influence our fashion: Punk, goth, hip-hop, rockabilly, and so many other looks are associated with specific musical styles. We might join bands, orchestras, or choirs, encircling ourselves with peers who share a common interest or background. We might swap mixtapes or playlists to show affection, or screen new acquaintances based on their tastes. Our language influences the music we listen to and vice versa. It's all a great big highway pileup of factors that determine who we are, who we want to be, and who we grow into (and out of).

We remember our adolescence and young adulthood disproportionately to the rest of our lives—a psychological phenomenon called the reminiscence bump. During this same period, puberty can make our emotions virtually explosive. The collision of these two phenomena means our hormone-addled brains document our most awkward years with laser-cut clarity. Music is, of course, tangled up in all of this. Its connection to emotion and memory means its impact on us is magnified during this volatile period. The reminiscence bump amplifies this impact and our emerging sense of self turns it into a sonic boom.

Whether we like the music or not is irrelevant. Hearing tracks and tunes from our teens and early twenties can be especially transportive. Do I truly love the collaborative work of Jennifer Lopez and Ja Rule? No. Does "I'm Real (Remix)" instantly pull me back in time to relive high school hijinks? Unfortunately, yes.

Other kinds of art, and other sensory experiences, can certainly conjure up our pasts—when I smell rosewater, I think of my mother; when I see a drawing of a robot, I think of my brother. But music manipulates our minds with singular power. The way we process it is not limited to the auditory cortex; it makes the brain fluoresce with activity. It connects the unconnected. It relaxes and excites. It shivers spines. It is therapy after a breakup; it helps heal after a stroke or traumatic brain injury. It triggers memories, and, in rare cases, hallucinations. Perhaps even older than humanity itself, encoded in our ancestors well before *Homo sapiens* slouched into existence. It sets fire to the lizard parts of our brains.

Music catalyzes both memory (as of a person, situation, event, place, or feeling) and nostalgia (a memory accompanied by desire or attempt to recreate or return to that state). The two are related but distinct; the latter is a function of the former. For example: Listening to J-Lo (ft. Ja Rule) will trigger a memory of an old friend, and I'll get in touch with that friend out of a sense of nostalgia. Memories are internal, unique to our own life experiences, and they belong only to us unless we express them. But nostalgia is a universal phenomenon—and like any universal human experience, capitalism grabs it by the throat and shakes it down.

Mass-distributed music, already heavily commercialized yet experienced on a deeply personal level by every listener, is an easy target for capitalization. Straightforward and profitable. Rereleases and remasters of albums, best-ofs, compilations—they're easy sells. Reunite Beyoncé with Destiny's Child, or Justin Timberlake with *NSYNC. Give them a reunion tour or a Super Bowl halftime show and you've got yourself a piggy bank to smash open. They could even reunite J-Lo and Ja Rule to make a quick buck, but they probably shouldn't.

The Los Angeles Philharmonic had barely hung up its coat at its new home at the Walt Disney Concert Hall—that silvery mishmash of deflating polyhedra designed by Frank Gehry—when it suddenly found itself party to a weird side-quest in the history of classical music: On May 10, 2004, it became the first-ever American orchestra to put on a concert of video game music. That concert, "Dear Friends – Music from Final Fantasy," featured Nobuo Uematsu's work exclusively (only one piece from *Final Fantasy VI* made the cut: Terra's theme). It's a testament to Uematsu's talent and popularity that his was the first video game music to pop up in a US symphony hall—and that it seeded an ecosystem of game music performance that thrives in America to this day.

Because the concept of video game music was hazy back then, especially for those older than late Gen-Xers and Millennials, because of its perceived intrusion into classical space, and because this was the first stateside concert of its kind, I will forgive 2004's critics for not knowing quite how to approach the "Dear Friends" concert. *The Los Angeles Times* said of it, in a headline that might have been written by Poochie—*The Simpsons*'s surfboarding dog wearing sunglasses and a backward ball cap—"Yow! This concert's got game." The *New York Times* review was entitled "Video Fantasy Replaces Mozart (But Who's Keeping

Score?)", a headline that does double duty: First, it is a very good joke about how the sheet music orchestras play from is referred to as a "score," and how a famous feature of video games is that they keep "score." Second, it lets us know that the person who wrote it may have played their first and last video game in the 80s, and that they did not know that FF games do no scorekeeping. "A decade ago," writes Matthew Mirapaul in the *New York Times*, "It would have been difficult to imagine that the beeping and whirring that accompanied most video games would have been worthy of the concert hall."

Fans were as enthusiastic about "Dear Friends" as critics were nonplussed. The concert sold out three days after it was announced and tickets were scalped on eBay at exorbitant prices. A review of the concert published on IGN included the words "wet dream," a rhetorical move rarely seen in reviews of classical music.

Questions about whether or not game music is "worthy" of performance in classical spaces swirled around "Dear Friends": Does game music have the same artistic merit as standard concert fare? Is its relationship with a commercial product a sacrilege? (How quickly critics forget that tug between art and commerce. Operas, after all, are productions meant to sell tickets, and the best seats can cost a small fortune.) In a pre-concert interview for Mirapaul's *New York Times* piece, one of the orchestra's flautists called Uematsu's music "completely without integrity" and "really cheesy." To each their own, I guess.

Questions about merit and integrity continue to swirl today, but mostly among critics and academics. The concerts are still happening, and they're not likely to go away anytime soon. McLellan, that sage of the square wave, never worried about game sound's worthiness—and once the rest of the classical community catches up to his 36-year-old opinion, they won't worry about it either.

One decade before "Dear Friends" hit the real-world concert stage, *FF6*'s Celes strode onto her 16-bit opera stage in living rooms across the world. Even before that—as far back as the mid-80s—video games were scored with memorable tunes that far surpassed the pejoratively termed "bleeps and bloops" that characterized the earliest electronic games. The music of Mario and Zelda lives and breathes even today, but the idea of game music as meaningless noise persisted in the popular imagination—or at least the imagination of adult music critics writing for major publications.

Symphonic performances of game music are common now, and they have made it to cultural capitals all over Europe, Asia, and the Americas. They've played Carnegie Hall, Royal Albert Hall, and the Sydney Opera House. One-off concerts became profitable tours—and the FF touring machine is unusually enduring and popular. There is still enormous demand for Uematsu's music, and that of his peers and their successors.

Today, Final Fantasy, Zelda, and Pokémon games all have their own concert tours, as do games published by Capcom; other tours are more ecumenical, drawing on sources from across consoles, publishers, and decades. Tickets sell so well—just as they did in 2004—that the concerts are sometimes hailed as the financial saviors of modern orchestras. They're credited with drawing younger, more diverse crowds to symphony halls, and for more than just the video game music concerts themselves. Come for the Mega Man, stay for the Mahler.

The idea seems so obvious now that one wonders why nobody thought of it sooner. After all, by the time "Dear Friends" came along, video games had been a phenomenon for more than two decades—and orchestras had been struggling with aging audiences, fundraising troubles, declining subscription sales, and other financial woes for at least as long. The delay in recognizing this opportunity can be blamed partly on the conservatism with which orchestras typically guide their programming. The old warhorses—Beethoven's Fifth or Ninth, Mozart's *Requiem*, Orff's *Carmina Burana*, and other instantly familiar repertoire—are usually judged to be the easiest sell, and they're also the most familiar to musicians. New music presents both an artistic and financial risk, and it takes a little more work—which is why orchestras continue to repeat, season after season, the same works of centuries-dead white men. I love pizza, folks, but I don't want to eat it for dinner every night.

If American artistic directors had been paying attention, they could have spotted a hot trend from a mile—well, five thousand miles—away.

•

Uematsu's "Dear Friends" was the first stateside performance of video game music by a major orchestra, but not the first one on the planet. On August 20, 1987, the Tokyo Strings Ensemble took the stage at Tokyo's Suntory Hall, where an enthusiastic audience of about two thousand had congregated to hear the world premiere of two symphonic suites composed and arranged by Koichi Sugiyama. Sugiyama's music had been buzzing in living rooms all over Japan for over a year—played by the Famicom and through TV speakers—as gamers wormed their ways through *Dragon Quest* (1986) and *Dragon Quest II* (1987). Sugiyama's suites were based on the music he had written for these games. It was billed as a "Family Classic Concert"—a "Famicon," if you will—welcoming children and adults alike, just as video games invited both to play as equals.

About two years later, on May 20, 1989, in the Gotanda district of Tokyo, members of the Tokyo

Symphony Orchestra took the stage at the 1,800-seat theatre U-Port Hall to play the world premiere of a seven-movement suite of music by Nobuo Uematsu (arranged by father-son duo Katsuhisa and Takayuki Hattori, and conducted by the former). This suite featured music from *FF1* and *FF2*, similar to the format of Sugiyama's concert two years earlier. It's not exactly idea theft—if you write music, you naturally want to see it performed. But it does reflect that tangled-up, borrow-for-keepsies relationship between DQ and FF, between Sugiyama and Uematsu.

In a 2009 interview with *Wired* magazine, Uematsu made the connection explicit: "In Japan, there had already been orchestral concerts of the music from DQ, and I realized that I could probably do a Final Fantasy one." That Uematsu was two years late did not matter. His music found success in America that Sugiyama's never did, just as FF prevailed over DQ in the West. Without *DQ1*, there would be no *FF1*—and implicit in the quote from Uematsu's *Wired* interview is that without the DQ suites, there might not have been a FF suite.

Remember that Uematsu hadn't planned game music to be his career; he'd wanted to move on to movies or pop songwriting. He'd never expressed an interest in classical music—and, even when he decided to put on his concert, he outsourced the orchestration and conducting to Messrs. Hattori. If he hadn't gotten the idea to perform his music from Sugiyama, would he have gotten the idea at all?

•

A 2015 album of arrangements of Uematsu's work, *Final Symphony*—based on the music of *FF6*, *FF7*, and *FF10*, and recorded by the London Symphony Orchestra under the direction of Eckehard Stier—topped the iTunes classical charts in at least ten countries and reached the top five on both the Billboard classical charts and the Official UK Charts. Uematsu himself has landed in the British radio station Classic FM's Hall of Fame six consecutive times, topping out at number 3 (of 300). His music has placed ahead of well-established and enduringly popular masterworks such as Vivaldi's *The Four Seasons*, Mozart's *The Marriage of Figaro* and *Eine kleine Nachtmusik*, and Handel's *Messiah*. The Hall of Fame is an unscientific poll, prone to a bit of organized campaigning, and specifically reflects the tastes of British listeners (Ralph Vaughan Williams, England's pride, seems to play an outsize role in the listings. He's not exactly a household name in the States.) But Uematsu's consistent placement on the list speaks to the enthusiasm of his fanbase.

How did this composer of music for video games—who, when he began working in the medium, was himself not sure of its potential for artistic expression—come to be so adored? And in such an exacting space as the classical music world? Why is it that his music isn't simply covered by a rock band with a small string section? Or by some new music ensemble equally as hard to genrefy as Uematsu's music itself? If the music isn't virtuosic (it isn't) and it's easily adaptable (it is), then why is it that it most popularly manifests as "classical?" Why does it demand a symphony hall?

Part of it may be due to that first performance in 1989, owed to Sugiyama's 1987 performance—Sugiyama who had already carved a respected place for himself in the Japanese music community. Another part of it is that, beginning in the 16-bit era, FF's music was arranged for a synthesized ensemble that vaguely resembles an orchestra—strings, woodwinds, horns. But that doesn't tell the whole story; plenty of other game music also speaks this language and isn't widely performed by orchestras. Something about FF's music reaches for the ritual of the orchestra tuning to the concert A, the formality of a conductor and a concertmaster.

Certainly, as technology grew more accommodating, Uematsu's music began to resemble classical music and film scores more literally, as with "One-Winged Angel," or *FF8*'s "Liberi Fatali," which shares the bombast of the "Dies irae" from Mozart's or Verdi's *Requiem*. But *FF6*'s opera scene—still humbled by its synthesizers and warbly diva—was the real inflection point, not just for the Final Fantasy series but for the way we think about video game music as a whole. This was the first time a video game sat the player down in the dress circle and said, "Shush. Listen."

•

After the second Dragon Quest suite ended to sustained applause and a lone "Bravo!", the orchestra moved on to Camille Saint-Saëns's well-loved *Le Carnaval des animaux*—another orchestral suite, this time with bona fide classical cred. (Come for the Sugiyama, stay for the Saint-Saëns.) *Carnaval* is a joy to listen to, and it's simple enough for children to love it, too. You might hear it played in an elementary school classroom. In one beloved 1962 recording of the piece, superstar composer-conductor-educator Leonard Bernstein punctuates his musicians' performance of the music with short, smoothly narrated passages that help children understand even better what they are about to hear. "My dear young friends," Bernstein says to begin the recording, "Music has lots of different uses in life."

Saint-Saëns was so worried that his silly, sweet *Carnaval* would detract from his "real" work that he refused to let it be published in his lifetime. What would the critics say? Would it be worthy of the concert hall? It was so much fun—would it be a cheap ploy to up ticket sales? But today it's his best-known work, probably because of its accessibility and familiarity. The very suite he worried would ruin his reputation now keeps it aloft. For a certain set of listeners, *Carnaval* references the wonder of childhood: watching a parade from dad's shoulders, mom taking us to see elephants at the zoo, the shimmer of tropical fish in an aquarium. For another set, the music of DQ and FF has the same effect—returning us from our swashbuckling to the living room rug, hitting pause and tossing the controller down when our parents call us to dinner.

•

Sugiyama's Family Concert was received well enough that a series of similar concerts followed, starting the slow march toward video game music's normalization as "art music." It's impossible to say how American audiences would have reacted if Sugiyama had brought his concerts to Los Angeles in the late 80s or early 90s. Given *DQ1*'s lackluster reception in the US, I doubt there would have been much reaction at all. I do know that, by the time I started dialing in to the internet in the mid-90s, a burgeoning community of video game music fans was already collecting and sharing game music online—fans who craved listening to their beloved music on demand.

Officially licensed soundtracks were available on CD in Japan in the 90s, but finding them in the US wasn't always easy. E-commerce, like everything else on the internet then, was still in its infancy. In the absence of Amazon.com, options for buying the albums online were limited. Since they weren't printed domestically, you'd have to rely on specialty import shops to stock them—and then you'd have to find the specialty shops that did. I still remember the triumph of stumbling into a weird import store—one that popped up in the disused leg of my local shopping mall—and seeing the soundtrack from *FF4* gleaming inside the glass case under the counter.

FF6 broke down this barrier to acquisition, allowing players to mail-order copies of the soundtrack by filling out a form that came in the game's official Nintendo player's guide, tucked in right next to that Moogle watch and ball cap. But it was still an expensive $39.99 plus a minimum $6.25 in shipping and handling (in 2021, this tops $80). The soundtrack to *Secret of Mana* was also for sale at a bargain-bin price of $17.99 (about $32 in 2021), shipping included. (As of this writing, *FF6*'s soundtrack is sold for $17.99 on the iTunes store—just about ten dollars in 1994—and streams for free on Spotify.)

Still, its appearance in the player's guide made it possible—easy, even—to buy the soundtrack. No weird import store in the haunted part of the mall needed, no cold dialing from the Yellow Pages. This was an early indicator of game music's commercial viability in North America. The soundtrack wouldn't have been offered for sale if there hadn't been a perceived market for it and it must have sold well enough, because later games had their soundtracks sold stateside as well. It shows foresight on the part of the game's American merchandising team, foresight Square may have lacked in the game's exclusionary, gendered marketing. They saw something special in Uematsu's score, and trusted that players would want to buy it after having played the game.

•

A curious inversion has taken place since the static of 70s arcade soundscapes. In the old days, sound was added to games by programmers without the help of composers. Because of a lack of know-how among early development teams, game music was likely to be a repurposed fragment of a familiar melody, sometimes programmed with an obvious lack of savoir faire. Starting with Koichi Sugiyama's 1987 concert, original tunes from video games began cropping up outside of arcades and living rooms. Today, you might even hear the soundtrack from a Legend of Zelda game playing as ambient music at a Starbucks. Now, with ample other technology available, contemporary musicians and game composers are returning to the sounds of 8- and 16-bit systems, drawing on their aesthetic but often flouting their technological limits. Game music started by parroting the familiar, but developed its own intelligence and variety with surprising speed. Once derivative, it is now derived from.

The perceived gap between "video game music" and "legitimate music" is closing. The handwringing of music critics, classical performers, and distinguished listeners is slowly being rendered moot. The synthesized has become real.

•

Adults around my age—Millennials—were once kids a controller cord's length away from the television. Many of us spent countless hours of our formative years exploring dungeons, beating bosses, collecting treasures, solving puzzles, and besting our friends' race times or high scores. We seek to remember these experiences, and sometimes to recreate that feeling of careless immersion. It might mean digging an old console out of the garage or visiting the gray internet to get an emulator and some ROMs. It might mean watching a short playthrough clip on YouTube or a Twitch stream. It might mean buying the mini rerelease of a classic console, or a modern third-party reengineering of one. It might mean listening to a soundtrack, going to the symphony, or digging up an old MIDI file.

Retailers, merchandisers, marketers—they know the power of nostalgia. They've commodified it. Businesses bank on it. And my generation isn't the first to fall for the ruse—nostalgia is the only explanation for *Mamma Mia!* or *A Very Brady Renovation*.

Film companies revive and reboot franchises that were practically dead and constantly refresh franchises that never quite went away—an endless barrage of Marvel, DC, King Kong, Planet of the Apes, Star Wars, James Bond, and Star Trek films. Video games do this too, making sure old characters and old games never die—maybe by adding a new title to a long-running series, or by repackaging and reselling an old favorite. Mario and Zelda and Mega Man aren't dead yet—and neither are their debut titles, *Super Mario Bros.*, The *Legend of Zelda*, or *Mega Man*. This tactic works: Adults rebuy and replay old games not just because they're fun, but because we remember playing them as kids and teens. Each rerelease of an old game presents an entry point for a new generation of players. For us, returning to an old favorite game means returning to a past version of ourselves; for new players, it means creating an experience to return to.

Where would Hot Topic be without intellectual properties developed in the 70s, 80s, 90s, and even 00s?

If climate change doesn't kill us first, humanity will die drowning in attitude tees and Funko Pops.

I can't speculate about how a game from 1994 might play to a generation who grew up with HDMI cables lying around, but games developed to look and play like games from 1994 (or earlier) have certainly made a comeback. An industry of pixelated, chiptuned games like *Shovel Knight* and *Stardew Valley* has sprung up and thrived in spite of technology that allows for much more detailed graphics and sound. 8- and 16-bit-ness has become its own visual and aural aesthetic. We never played *Shovel Knight* games as kids, but we feel like we're creating a childhood memory *ex post facto*; it conjures all those summers we spent callusing up our thumbs. It's neoclassicism for video games: Its existence both indicates and contributes to the continued appeal of the classical.

You probably won't find FF-branded candy at your local gas station—not in the US, anyway—but the series still capitalizes on a collective, nostalgia-fueled affinity. It has had innumerable spin-offs, sequels, serials, remasters, and rereleases, sometimes with questionable results. After its initial release on the SNES in 1994, *FF6* was rereleased on the PlayStation in 1999, then in a this-program-has-been-formatted-to-fit-your-screen version on the Game Boy Advance in 2007, then as a digital title for the Wii and PlayStation 3. More recently (and most regrettably) it was remastered for Android, iOS, and Windows. It also contributed, at least in part, to the sales frenzy surrounding the Super NES Classic Edition, a bona fide nostalgia machine preloaded with popular games from the 90s.

It's easy to find a way to replay an old FF game, but the series—despite its immense success and continued demand—hasn't made quite the merchandising splash in the US that other properties have. ("NO WIMPS.") Some plushies, t-shirts, and action figures are available for sale on Square Enix's website, but FF isn't usually in the aforementioned tub full of t-shirts at Hot Topic, nor does it have a heavy presence in Hot Topic's inventory, nor has it developed a franchise of blockbuster films. (The first major theatrically released film flopped.) But the series's music has made up for the lack of merchandise in a curiously effective way.

FF's music fuels more than just ticket sales. Audience members who grew up playing the games may want to rebuy and replay one after seeing its music in concert and concertgoers who are new to the series might be compelled enough by the music to give one of the games a try. (I'd never played a Phoenix Wright game until after I heard some of its music played in concert.) With each concert, each rerelease, each MIDI transcription, and each fan-made YouTube performance, old ties to the series are renewed and new ones are formed or strengthened. With each ticket, each download, each click, profits inch up, directly or indirectly. As audiences grow, so does the budget to sell. Final Fantasy's music is one cog in—and the inexhaustible energy source of—a perpetual nostalgia machine.

•

FF6 revolves around its characters, but that's not how Nobuo Uematsu worked to build the game's score. "I just wrote as the tracks came to me," he told me in an email. "[Then] I'd simply decide which melodies worked for which characters." I was stunned to learn this. The character themes—those which fit so perfectly with their subjects—were retrofitted! "The vast majority of a composer's work," he continued, "is to make decisions."

Uematsu didn't give me any details about the decision-making process—just that it happened. I would expect him to have read the script, thoughtfully selected the music he'd created, and possibly rework parts of it to fit each character, each situation. I know that for later games, he did some of this. But for all I know, *FF6* could be thrown darts—each one a bullseye.

I considered this all very seriously as I wrote this book. I'd already done a lot of analysis and writing, and Uematsu's cavalier response to my question shook me up. I remembered Roland Barthes's theory that the intent of the artist is immaterial; it's the interpretation of the audience that matters. So, in a way, meaning is retrofitted: Terra's music characterizes her; if she had had different music, she would have been a different character. Similarly, if Terra's music had been used for another character, I'd have picked it apart in a much different way. The same goes for every other character, and every other piece of music, in *Final Fantasy VI*.

As listeners, it isn't our work to divine what the artist must have been thinking. Sometimes it can be enlightening to hear from them about their process, but ultimately, we are the deciders of meaning. We all do this work differently because we come with different ears, different brains, different backgrounds, and different ideas. Music hits us all in different ways, and some of us it doesn't hit at all.

There are certain truths or facts in this book—dates and figures, bits of history, scraps and diagrams of music. But the rest—what music says about a character, what the relationship of two pieces of music means, how to interpret a piece's dramatic effect, why a half-hour spent in a 256-color opera house is so important—that's all tea leaves and sheep guts. You could listen and think and write and come up with something completely different. You can hate this entire soundtrack and all of my ideas about it, and that's OK, too. Hating is also part of the work of consuming art and media, of being critics for ourselves.

It's not necessarily nostalgia to revisit art. It's work. It's a form of study, a critical decision, an expression of appreciation. It's part of our human desire to be moved, to transcend.

•

Uematsu's skill is such that, in the early to mid-90s, swaths of us played and replayed the games he scored without ever tiring of his work. A community of us took it upon ourselves to record, arrange, and share his music online when we couldn't get it anywhere else. He had been buzzing in our living rooms, bedrooms, and dorm rooms for almost fifteen years, and we were still starved enough of his music to rush to the symphony hall. He largely—almost single-handedly—changed the way Americans interact with game music. He has made a firm impression among scholars and practitioners of music. Most extraordinarily, he managed to reach across the globe and subtly manipulate the minds of millions of gamers. With a simple musical gesture, he effects a collective catch in our throats, or a pit in our stomachs, or a skip in our heartbeats. All with sensitivity, all with specificity, all with just the right timing—all in service of stories he didn't write, but which he nonetheless owns.

A side gig ended up changing the world. He, a man with no formal training, who hadn't planned to stick around, has accomplished something few musicians ever have: He has heard us speak his name.

I asked Nobuo Uematsu what job he would like to have had if he hadn't become a musician. He said simply, "A poet." This tracks: Nowhere outside poetry is the divide between intent and interpretation so obvious. Nowhere else must an artist work so hard to craft something so concrete with such an ephemeral toolkit. Nowhere else, I think, than music.

In 2011, another interviewer asked Uematsu the very same question, and his answer wasn't "poet." It was "pro wrestler."

•

After Uematsu's character medley, after the heroes complete their escape from Kefka's tower, after the credits finish rolling, after the Falcon streaks across the sky, leaving a wake of two thin clouds, "The End" appears on the screen in letters formed by rippling water. Then there's silence.

Your heart might still be pounding from the battle with Kefka after the music has wrapped up, or you may be unsure what to do with yourself after sinking a full workweek of hours into a game. You just sit there and stare. After twenty seconds, Uematsu's familiar prelude starts to twinkle on its harp. Onscreen, stars begin to whiz past you as if you're flying through space, into the unknown.

Only the words say "The End." Water ripples outward with seeming endlessness. There is no friction in space; you can travel the stars forever. And a prelude is a beginning.

NOTES

All musical figures in this book were prepared by the author using the US release of the game's soundtrack, *Kefka's Domain*, as a reference. Track names in this book are taken from this release.

An email interview with Nobuo Uematsu was conducted in October 2017 in Japanese, with assistance from translator Taku Watanabe and Boss Fight Books editor Michael P. Williams.

Primordial Bloop

Joseph McLellan's "Pac-Man Overture in G-Whiz" was published in the *Washington Post* on January 7, 1983: https://wapo.st/3qwqmdo.

Paul McCartney cites the influence of John Cage on the Beatles' "Revolution 9" in Vanessa Thorpe's article "Forty years on, McCartney wants the world to hear 'lost' Beatles epic," published at the Guardian on November 15, 2008: https://bit.ly/3kXrju0.

Andrew Schartmann's book, *Koji Kondo's Super Mario Bros. 3 Soundtrack*, was published by Bloomsbury Academic in 2015 as part of their 33 ⅓ series.

The reported number of copies of *Dragon Quest* (released as *Dragon Warrior*) given away by *Nintendo Power* vary by source. According to Press the Buttons's August 28, 2014 piece "How Did Nintendo Handle The Great Dragon Warrior Giveaway?," video game historian Frank Cifaldi notes "thousands," and fellow historian Steve Lin offers evidence of *Nintendo Power* staff receiving "70,000 [redemption] cards per hour" (https://bit.ly/3t1Tafm). David Oxford's "Howard Phillips Speaks on Dragon Quest's Initial Performance and Nintendo Power Giveaway," published March 29, 2018 by *Old School Gamer Magazine*, reports that Phillips recalls the number given away as somewhere between 500,000 and one million copies (https://bit.ly/30pZiBX).

A rough Japanese language timeline of Koichi Sugiyama's professional history formerly appeared on his official website Sugiyama Koichi no Sekai (sugimania.com). A 2011 snapshot is available at the Internet Archive: https://bit.ly/38pmTHe.

Nick Rox and K. Lee described Nobuo Uematsu as "godlike" in their review of *FF6* in *Diehard Gamefan* magazine, vol. 2, no, 10 (October 1994), archived at the Internet Archive: https://bit.ly/2OjYLPt.

Uematsu's interview with the Red Bull Music Academy Daily was conducted by Nick Dwyer and posted on October 2,

2014 as "Interview: Final Fantasy's Nobuo Uematsu": https://win.gs/3esR3x1.

Further information on Uematsu's musical upbringing is revealed in a series of video interviews conducted in 2007 by 1UP's James Mielke called "A Day in the Life of Nobuo Uematsu," compiled and uploaded to YouTube as "1up/James Mielke Interviews Nobuo Uematsu" (https://youtu.be/t1QPNZ_bzlE). Mielke's write-up and the full text of the interview was originally posted to 1UP on February 15, 2008, and can be found at the Internet Archive: https://bit.ly/3bxwE8a.

Some critical background on Wolfgang Amadeus Mozart was published in the fifth edition of *Grove's Dictionary of Music and Musicians*, edited by Eric Blom (Macmillan/St. Martin's Press, 1954). Relevant passages on pages 950-951 of volume 5 of the dictionary are available at the Internet Archive: https://bit.ly/38lPugw

The White Stripes documentary *Under Great White Northern Lights* was directed by Emmett Malloy and released in 2009.

Igor Stravinsky's *Poétique musicale sous forme de six leçons* was first published in French by Harvard University Press in 1942. It was translated as *Poetics of Music in the Form of Six Lessons* in 1947.

Uematsu cites various musical genres and artists as influences on his style depending on the source. According to a panel interview at Otakon 2011 reported by I-hsiu Lin of the Journal of the Lincoln Heights Literary Society, one was prog rock (https://bit.ly/2O9BrUE). He cited ABBA in an interview with *Weekly Famitsu* which translated to English by Sachi Coxon of RPGamer (https://bit.ly/3cbhuEM). He named Tchaikovsky as another to John Olin of Xbox Evolved, as reported by the unofficial fan site nobuouematsu.com (https://bit.ly/3v8UGOt), and also to the audience of Anime Boston 2010, as reported by Square Enix Music Online (https://bit.ly/30uPrdS). Elton John's album *Honky Château* was listed as an influence in his interview with Nick Dwyer at the Red Bull Music Academy Daily. And he references Keith Urban by way of his band The Ranch in an interview conducted by Bob Rork (https://bit.ly/3cfbv1Q).

Uematsu's interview where he recalled his beginnings at SquareSoft was conducted by Eric Steffens of Paladin Entertainment in February 1999, and is currently available via the Internet Archive: https://bit.ly/3rBdcwM.

Uematsu's interview in which he revealed he "struggled to produce originality in the same three tones" was Matthew Belinkie's "Video game music: not just kid stuff," originally posted December 15, 1999 and available at VGMusic, the Video Game Music Archive: https://bit.ly/3t54pDP.

Uematsu's 1994 interview where he discusses rhythm and melody was originally published in Japanese in the book *Gēmu Dezainā Nyūmon* ("Introduction to Game Design") by Shibao Eirei and Kasai Osamu (Shōgakukan, 1994). It is available in English through Shmuplations's 1994 Game Developers Interview Collection: https://bit.ly/2Oalw8y.

The Zeroth Half

Some of Kefka's expanded backstory was revealed in the Japanese book *Fainaru Fantajī VI Settei Shiryō-hen* ("*Final Fantasy VI* Setting Materials Guide"), published by NTT Publishing in 1994. An English translation is available at the Final Fantasy Wiki at the talk page for Kefka: https://bit.ly/3c9tbM0.

Uematsu's interview with *Edge* magazine was published in issue 125 (March 2015) as "The Making of *Final Fantasy VI*." The text is currently available online at GamesRadar+: https://bit.ly/3rJW0Fm.

Hironobu Sakaguchi remarked on how a cast of more than twenty characters were combined into fourteen in a Japanese-language interview with *V-Jump* magazine (May 1994). The text was hosted at the Nobuo Uematsu Fansite: https://bit.ly/3enUxRn.

Chris Kohler's book *Power Up: How Japanese Video Games Gave the World an Extra Life* (BradyGames, 2004) reports how Uematsu was brought on to help complete *Chrono Trigger*'s soundtrack.

FF6's soundtrack was released in Japan on March 25, 1994 by NTT Publishing as *Final Fantasy VI Original Soundtrack*. The US release by Square came on July 1, 1994, titled as *Kefka's Domain*.

Uematsu revealed that "he could start experimenting for the first time" with *FF6* in Luke Karmali's feature "Nobuo Uematsu

Remembers 20 Years of Final Fantasy Soundtracks," first published December 19, 2014 at IGN: https://bit.ly/3l6xuM9.

Ryan Thompson compares *FF6* to an opera in an audio interview with Classical MPR's Emily Reese of the podcast Top Score, published on July 30, 2015 as "A musicologist's look at '*Final Fantasy VI*'": https://bit.ly/3erpkgc.

FF6 reviews were sources from contemporary publications: Danyon Carpenter's review in the October 1994 issue of *Electronic Gaming Monthly*; Scary Larry's review in "Role Player's Realm," published in *GamePro* vol. 6, no. 11 (aka number 64, November 1994) (https://bit.ly/3t7oFVh); the November 1994 issue of *Game Informer*; and *Nintendo Power*, number 65.

For a particularly epic takedown of *FF6*'s merits, see iovandrake's March 8, 2012 post "Why is this game so overrated?" in the GameFAQs forum: https://bit.ly/38qzytC.

Game Informer ranked *FF6* as #2 of their "Top 100 RPGs of All Time" in issue 290 (June 2017). The list was published online on January 1, 2018 (https://bit.ly/3coP6yW). RPGFan ranked *FF6* as #1 in the "Best Final Fantasy Games - Mainline Titles," part of a larger "The Best (and Worst) Final Fantasy Games" feature from April 8, 2011 (https://bit.ly/3cobEA3). Jason Schreier placed it as #1 in "Let's Rank The *Final Fantasy* Games, Best to Worst," published to Kotaku on January 29, 2013 (https://bit.ly/3qEN6b0). IGN also placed it as #1 in their May 5, 2016 "Ranking the Final Fantasy Games" where it was blurbed by Marty Sliva (https://

bit.ly/3vgmFfw). Anthony John Agnello of GamesRadar+ placed it as #1 in his "The 25 best Final Fantasy games," published February 22, 2017 (https://bit.ly/2N49JI6). Jeremy Parish's "Ranking the numbered Final Fantasy games," published at Polygon on December 19, 2017 also ranks it as #1 (https://bit.ly/3epIRxt). Damien Lykins of Screen Rant similarly placed it as #1 in "25 Greatest Final Fantasy Games Of All Time, Officially Ranked," published on February 10, 2019 (https://bit.ly/2PO0pJr). It was at the top of Devin "Hellbird" Rigotti's "Every numbered Final Fantasy series ranked worst to best," published February 17, 2020 to RedBull.com (https://win.gs/38tB1iA). And last up—and yet *FF6* still first on!—Steven Petite's "The best Final Fantasy games, ranked from best to worst," which was first published in Digital Trends in 2020 (https://bit.ly/3v7Hv0t).

Yoshinori Kitase's interview with Edge, "The Making Of: *Final Fantasy VI*," was published on August 5, 2013. It is currently available through the Internet Archive: https://bit.ly/3l6mmyQ.

Uematsu declared that *FF6* was his favorite Final Fantasy game at the 2011 Otakon panel and reported by the Journal of the Lincoln Heights Literary Society.

Kirk Hamilton's "What It's Like to Play *Final Fantasy VI* for the First Time" was published at Kotaku on August 27, 2015: https://bit.ly/30KdRk1.

For examples of other critical books written about *FF6* other than the present volume, see for instance Pierre Maugein's *La légende Final Fantasy VI: Création, univers, décryptage* (Third

Éditions, 2015) and Patrick Holleman's *Reverse Design: Final Fantasy VI* (CRC Press, 2018).

Sales numbers for the Final Fantasy series were sourced from the Video Game Sales Wiki entry: https://bit.ly/2OK8hel.

Sakaguchi laments *FF6*'s lukewarm sales in his interview with Jason Schreier, published as "Things Are Very Different For The Creator Of Final Fantasy" to Kotaku on September 2, 2014: https://bit.ly/3t7V4LA.

Technical specifications of the SNES's color palette are documented in the Wikipedia entry for the system: https://bit.ly/30Ad8Bu.

Kitase's comments on "mere ciphers for fighting" come from his 2013 interview with Edge, "The Making Of: *Final Fantasy VI*."

Noun Music

The ages of *FF6* characters are recorded in *Final Fantasy Ultimania Archive*, volume 1 (Dark Horse Books, 2018).

A 1914 English translation of Wang Wei's poem "Deer Park" by John C. Ferguson is recorded (and critiqued somewhat harshly) by Herbert A. Giles in "Another Mistranslator" in his Adversaria Sinica, series II, no. 1 (Shanghai: Kelly & Walsh, 1915):

> In the lone hills men are not seen
> Only the sound of their voices is heard.

The fading light enters the deep forest.
The reflection is on the green moss.

Giles provides his own translation which varies slightly from Ferguson's: https://bit.ly/38tBaCE. Even more variations can be found in Eliot Weinberger and Octavio Paz's *19 Ways of Looking at Wang Wei: How a Chinese Poem is Translated*, first published by Moyer Bell Limited in 1987, and later expanded in 2016 with "more ways" added.

Uematsu stated that Relm is his favorite *FF6* character in his May 1994 *V-Jump* magazine interview (preserved in Japanese at the Nobuo Uematsu Fansite).

KWhazit's alternate English translation of *FF6*'s script, as well as the original Japanese transcription along with Woolsey's translation, are laid out at KWhazit Oddities: https://bit.ly/3l5adu3.

Leitmotif

Wikipedia lists the total times of the Lord of the Rings trilogy's theatrical releases as 558 minutes, and clocks the Hobbit trilogy at 474 total minutes, a total of 1,032 minutes for the entire series. By contrast, the Met's 2018–2019 season estimates the runtimes for the *Ring Cycle* operas as follows: *Rheingold* (150 mins, without intermission); *Walküre* (295 minutes, with two intermissions), *Siegfried* (306 minutes, with two intermissions); *Götterdämmerung* (332 minutes, with two intermissions). Their net total is 1,082 minutes, giving Wagner's opus just slightly over one more hour of content than Peter Jackson's Tolkien adaptation.

Maria and Draco

The TV commercial featuring the claymation Moogle was uploaded to YouTube on September 28, 2009 as "*Final Fantasy III* - Commercial" by HerofTime64: https://youtu.be/d15qmRzn2Pc.

Nintendo Power's magazine-length strategy guide for the game was *Final Fantasy III: Nintendo Player's Guide* published in 1994.

The "It doesn't seem fair, does it?"/"Who says life is fair?" ad campaign is documented as "*Final Fantasy VI* - Propaganda" at RPGamer: https://bit.ly/2OHZ3PO.

Yoshitaka Amano's concept of art of Moogles can be found in various places, such as *The Sky: The Art of Final Fantasy* (Dark Horse, 2013), the first volume of Dark Horse's *Final Fantasy Ultimania Archive*, *Final Fantasy III: Nintendo Player's Guide*, and in the game's manual.

William Cheng's *Sound Play: Video Games and the Musical Imagination* was published by Oxford University Press in 2014. Of particular note is chapter 2, "How Celes Sang."

The Cutting Room Floor's wiki entry for *FF6* reveals several opera-related items cut from the game: https://bit.ly/3l4uKis.

Nostalgitek Factory

Chris Pasles's "Yow! This concert's got game" was published in the *Los Angeles Times* on April 4, 2004: https://lat.ms/3qA-oqAC. Matthew Mirapaul's "Video Fantasy Replaces Mozart (But Who's Keeping Score?)" was published in the *New York Times* on May 10, 2004: https://nyti.ms/3lczXoE. Marc Nix's "wet dream" review was "Dear Friends: Music from Final Fantasy," published to IGN on May 11, 2004: https://bit.ly/3emQ95g.

Uematsu's interview with Chris Kohler, "An Evening With Uematsu, Final Fantasy's Music Man," was published at *Wired* on July 21, 2009: https://bit.ly/3etB2Xx, and is republished in the Boss Fight Books anthology, *Nightmare Mode*.

News of Uematsu's placement in the Classic FM's Hall of Fame was reported on their website in "Here's how Nobuo Uematsu changed the course of classical music with his Final Fantasy score," published on June 10, 2019: https://bit.ly/30xKW2o.

Uematsu revealed his alternative career track of "pro wrestler" in his 2011 Otakon panel reported by the Journal of the Lincoln Heights Literary Society.

ACKNOWLEDGEMENTS

This book happened because of the love and generosity of a city's worth of people. My gratitude to:

Nobuo Uematsu. Thank you for your time, and for the love you put into your art.

My editors, Gabe Durham and Mike Williams. Thank you for putting your faith in me and never losing it. Thank you for all you did to make this book.

Meghan Burklund, Matthew LeHew, Joseph M. Owens, Philip J. Reed, and Nick Sweeney. Thank you for reading this and for your invaluable input.

Christopher Moyer for laying this book out, and Cory Schmitz for designing the cover. Your work blesses this mess.

Taku Watanabe. Thank you for translating and making so many important sources accessible.

To everyone from the Deaf and Hard of Hearing gaming community who provided their input so readily when I asked, and to the memory of Susan Banks.

Rebecca Berbel, Kylene King, Jeremy Bent, and Curtis Retherford. Thank you for reading this in such a sorry state, and for unsorrying it.

Jolly and John Stewart. I wouldn't have a voice without you.

Margo Jefferson. Thank you for your wisdom, and for unknowingly giving me a backbone.

Matt Shafeek, Mary Jean Murphy, and Liz Walters, for your friendship, for the melted cheese, and for reading this as it evolved. Special thanks to Shafeek, for encouraging me to pitch.

Nick Toti, for your infuriating thoughts and ideas.

Josh Hefti, for the late-night playthroughs fueled by Surge™. I write this in the least sexual way possible: I will forever treasure our time on your waterbed.

Erica Flanagan, Tavern Wench, Goody Butterface, for the hours watching me play video games when we were kids, then listening to me talk about them for the rest of our lives.

My brothers, Stu, Steve, and Sean, for sometimes ceding the controller. And to Kevin and Jake. It's not germane to this book, but I did beat *Chrono Trigger*. I got it on video. It's in print.

My husband, Brett. Thank you for listening to, consoling, prodding, and advising me from the very first time I thought about writing as a vocation. Until the stars fall: Brett, I love you.

To the significant other of every person I've ever spoken to, all of whom knew *Final Fantasy VI* and got excited about this book.

Fuck. Who else.

SPECIAL THANKS

For making our fifth season of books possible, Boss Fight Books would like to thank John Romero, Ian Chung, Fenric Cayne, Trey Adams, Jennifer Durham-Fowler, Cathy Durham & Ed Locke, Ken Durham & Nancy Magnusson Durham, Nate Mitchell, Lawliet Tamaki Aivazis, Cassandra Newman, seanz0r, Zach Davis, Andrew "Xestrix" Carlson, Ant'ny Fataski, David Goodenough, Adam Hejmowski, Joshua Mallory, and Sean 'Ariamaki' Riedinger. Adam Rosenfield, Sileem Farghaly, Samuel Rauhala, mceaton, Nathan Tolf, brazzell dazzell, Todd Hansberger, Michael O'Leary, Connor Wack, Wes Locher, Yoan Sebdoun-Manny, Scott Mendenko, Jeff H, John Simms, Matthew LeHew, Aaron Murray, Jason 'XenoPhage' Frisvold, Kevin Foss, Mickey Possingham, Chris Suellentrop, Tim Suter, Yannick Rochat, Salvatore Pane, Anonymous, Josh Scherping, Joseph De Maria, J. Kyle Pittman, Bear Belcastro, Stephen Trinh, Shane Culp, Marc Beavan, Nik Zeltzer, Graham Guletz, Jonathan Charles Bruce, Samuel Kossow, Chris Furniss, Morgie73, David Altman, Dave Kapell, Justin "Vextalon" Brissette,

Greg Trawinski, David M. P. Goncalves, Nick DiNuzzo, Alex Rhys, Christopher Vermilya, Jim Fingal, Gavin Craig, Andrew S. Rosenfeld, Ryan Markel, John Hague, William Linn, Greg Cashman, Eric Pidkameny, Alasker, Meghan and Ethan Kaye, Allen Murray, Empty Clip Studios, Mark Freeman, Emerson Emser, James Terry, Kathryn Hemmann, Russell Wiley, Josh Lee, Gavin Graf, douglas riggs, utcv, Corey Losey, Kenny J. Murray, Wesley James Kevin Starr, Philip J Reed, Patrick Tenney, Caleb J. Ross, Victor Romero, Graham Faught, Victor Hunter, Rob Watkins, Stephen Milligan, Eric Tran, Jason Morales, Shawn Clark, Bobby Brankiewicz, Ric Peavyhouse, David Warden, Collin Johnson, Dash Reid, Jason Switzer, Mitchel Labonté, David Portnov, Ashli T., Javy Gwaltney, Royce Rezendes, Andrew Ferguson, Anthony McDonald, Seth Henriksen, Ben Rathert, Patrick Polk, Donald Hopkins, Matthew Millsap, Nate L., Sean Flannigan, Michael Scuderi, vilmibm, Black Lives Matter, John Olson, Malachi Dean Royer, Rusty Collins, Brett Bicksler, Nick Chaimov, Connor Bourn, Nathan Penland, Brayden Egan, Ken Nagasako, Matt Bell, Chris Price, Tamara Henderson, NESJumpman, Ryan Myers, licensetobill, Chris Davis, Nick Henderson, Michael Andrews Dr. Omar Zeid, Samuel DeSarno, Ceth Stifel, Rob H, Heath Bsharah, CK Malone, GigaSeifer, Nick Eliopulos, John Pope, Kyle Hall, Jordan Keith Albaugh, Some Other 1, Steven Vondra II, Bobby Burton, Alvin Yates, Marisa Henriquez, Sam Moseley, Jamie Perez,

Anthony de Jesus, Marq Casarez, Ross Stinemetz, JScott, Eric Wei, Diane Lane, David E., Bryan Mitchell, Kenneth Valentine, Nick Greer, Denham Harry, John Briski, John Boulmetis, Tim Aubel, Armand Tamzarian, B Young, Will Cross, Rob Schmuck, Giovanni Colantonio, Joline, Autumn Beauchesne, Wikipoem.org, Nicholas Limon | @AdventNick, mikecheb, Kelly Ziemski, Tomio Ueda, David Sekowski, Matthew J Riddle, Nick Blesch Clark, Casey Lawler, Mike Davis Jr., Deaven, Mike VK, Justin LaQuay, Jonathan Blue, Zowen, Evgeny Petrov, Brett King, David W. Hill, Ryan F. Feuerhelm, Kristian Watts, Michael Alfieri, Evan Turner, Jonathon Toft-Nielsen, Trevor Starkey, Gregory Lee Englander, TJ Michael, Maxi Organ, J. Asher Henry, D.Dust, James K., Kristen Maloney, Nicole Amato, Patrick King, Geoff McLaughlin, Keegan Chua, Michael Strickland, Dustin Meadows, Aram Kuredjian, thatwhichis, Supercade, Antti Rasanen, Sadozai, Trevor Rodenberger, Philippe Lupien, Bastien Gorissen, Nick Nelson, Andrew Griffin, Matthew Lemay, Hussain Alj, Jay K., John Thomas, Daniel E. Davis (Chainsaw), Keith Travis, Tristan Powell, Joel Bergman, Andy Johnson, Will Salsman, Phil Peterson, Chris Suzuki, Benjamin Hirdler, Joshua Carpenter, Youth in Decline, Zack Johnson, Zac Lovoy, Shannon McCormick, Mark D. Sullivan, and César Augusto Rivera P.

ALSO FROM
BOSS FIGHT BOOKS